THE BEETLE BOOK

D1726033

(Volkswagen of America, Inc.)

Other Books by Louis William Steinwedel

GUIDE TO GUNS AND HUNTING

THE MERCEDES-BENZ STORY

THE DUESENBERG

THE GUN COLLECTORS' FACT BOOK

THE GOLDEN AGE OF SPORTS CARS

THE BEETLE BOOK

America's 30-Year Love Affair with the "Bug"

by Louis William Steinwedel

PRENTICE-HALL, INC., Englewood Cliffs, New Jersey

Book Designer: Linda Huber
Art Director: Hal Siegel

The Beetle Book: America's 30-Year Love Affair With the "Bug"
by Louis William Steinwedel
Copyright © 1981 by Louis William Steinwedel
Address inquiries to Prentice-Hall, Inc.,
Englewood Cliffs, N.J. 07632
Printed in the United States of America
Prentice-Hall International, Inc., London
Prentice-Hall of Australia, Pty. Ltd., Sydney
Prentice-Hall of Canada, Ltd., Toronto
Prentice-Hall of India Private Ltd., New Delhi
Prentice-Hall of Japan, Inc., Tokyo
Prentice-Hall of Southeast Asia Pte. Ltd., Singapore
Whitehall Books Limited, Wellington, New Zealand

10   9   8   7   6   5   4   3   2   1

Library of Congress Cataloging in Publication Data
Steinwedel, Louis William.
  The Beetle book.
  Includes index.
  1. Volkswagen automobile.   I. Title.
TL215.V6S78   629.2'222   81-2754
                        AACR2
ISBN 0-13-071316-3
ISBN 0-13-071308-2 (PBK)

(Thoroughbred Cars, Inc.)

Contents

THE BEETLE BOOK
is dedicated to
Ralph and Frankie Brocato

(Volkswagen of America, Inc.)

(Volkswagen of America, Inc.)

Introduction

The story of the Volkswagen Beetle has most of the elements that would have interested the Brothers Grimm in constructing a new fairy tale: a sorcerer who could spin gold out of straw (or at least a good car out of dreams and promises, which is about the same thing); an evil king (substitute mad dictator); the woodsman, noble of spirit, who saves the day through courage and hard work (substitute corporate administrator); and even a pot of gold at the end of the rainbow. The only hitch is that the hero stays an ugly little frog and still wins the princess. . . . So where is it graven in stone that ugly little frogs, or even Beetles, can't get a princess every now and then?

In the whole history of industrial design there has never been anything quite like the Volkswagen Beetle. There have been epic machines endowed with the endurance to keep doing their jobs with a regal disregard for the calendar; Colt's single-action army revolver of 1873, Hoover's "beat and sweep" vacuum, and McDonnell Douglas's DC-3 come to mind. But no mechanical entity can equal the record of the homely Beetle; no industrial design has ever been so intensely developed and improved and yet remained so visually similar and faithful to its original purpose as the Volkswagen. The first and last (whenever its day may come) Beetles will share shape, concept, and remarkably similar appearance.

The Wolfsburg plant produced its first Beetle on August 15, 1940. It was bombed nearly to oblivion in the next few years, yet built some of the world's first postwar new cars—some 1,785 of them by the end of 1945. Improvement of the Beetle continued simultaneously with its struggles to survive, and as early as 1953 not a single screw matched those used in the prototype model. The Beetle established itself as the basic transport from Antarctica to the Amazon to Los Angeles. By the 1960s it was a legitimate institution, as familiar a shape on this planet, those VW ads told us, as Coca-Cola bottles. On February 17, 1972, the car which a Ford executive in 1948 pronounced "not worth a damn" broke the production record of the landmark Model T with the assembly of the 15,007,034th Beetle.

But the appeal of the Beetle was not so much that it ran in blizzards, deserts, swamps, and on freeways without water and with very little fuel, that it was cheap to buy, or that it threatened to last forever. Its appeal was its *appeal*. It had a gut-level magnetism, a somewhat mysterious, almost psychic attraction to an astonishingly wide spectrum of people. It was simultaneously the transport of the flower-bedecked counterculture and of William Buckley, Mrs. Cornelius Vanderbilt Whitney, Paul Newman, and Princess Margaret. People who could not agree on art, politics, literature, or life-style found common ground in a homely little automobile appropriately called the "people's car." If all its other virtues—and vices—are forgotten, at least *that* deserves to be remembered.

1/A Volks-Gallery

(Unless otherwise indicated all photos are courtesy of Krishman Photographic Service.)

(Volkswagen of America, Inc.)

Delusions of grandeur . . .

WOB-VT 27

. . . or of pathos.

5—4—3—2—1—Zero. Blast off! (Volkswagen of America, Inc.)

Pursuits in relay? (Volkswagen of America, Inc.)

Oh, I just can't bear these little cars.
(Volkswagen of America, Inc.)

There are Beetle freaks and there are jogging freaks. And then . . .
(Volkswagen of America, Inc.)

Keep on bugging—er, trucking.

13

Overcompensator. *(Small World)*

For reasons probably only Dr. Freud would understand, some people are unusually fascinated with rear ends of Volkswagens.

Some strange fetishes have resulted, roughly divided into the pessimists . . .

14

. . . and the optimists,

while others appear to exhibit slight schizoid tendencies, unable to choose between the Bug and the Box, interbreeding with other species.

It's all a matter of personal expression.

19

"De gustibus non est disputandum," said the lady as she kissed the cow.

Indoor-outdoor carpet covered.

20

Gilding the lily; the caterpillar
becomes a bug—er, butterfly.

The ingenuity of VW owners knoweth no bounds.

Backseat driver's delight. (Volkswagen of America, Inc.)

The ads say, "Think small";
so I thought smaller.

Lunar lander? Brush buggy? Transistorized rapid-transit prototype?

More improvisations on a common theme.

The end . . .

. . . But not quite.

Prophecy.

2/A Beetle Genealogy

The astrologer consulted the stars; he ran his finger among the charts of his ephemeris, and checked the coordinates of longitude and latitude. He calculated, he meditated, and then he began to write the horoscope of Herbie von Volkswagen, born in Stuttgart, Germany, on the twenty-fifth of September, 1931:

"A lover of people, gregarious, at home with 'the folks' . . . good-natured, pleasant . . . intelligent, well-reasoned, but can be naive . . . sometimes inconsistent but able to merge the great and the small, to synthesize extremes with inborn Libran sense of balance; an admirer of harmony . . . the ability to remain mild-mannered but determined in the face of duty . . . a marked preference for soft curves over

Ferdinand Porsche's earliest recognition as an innovative engineer who "put the power where it is used" came from this Lohner electric car of 1900, which was powered by separate electric motors in the front wheels. A later version used a Daimler internal-combustion engine to generate power for the twin electric motors, and the car reached 55 mph. (Volkswagen of America, Inc.)

sharp angles . . . industrious, an assiduous worker . . . moves through life with a healthy regularity . . . honest, not given to extravagant promise or image."

He came of good lineage, no doubt about that. His ancestors included a combination gas engine/electric vehicle so reliable that it became the world's first motorized fire engine in 1904, one of the earliest airplane engines (and with

When Porsche became technical director at Austro-Daimler in 1905, one of his early products was the Mercedes *Mixt*, a combination electric/internal-combustion car which was fast and reliable. (Volkswagen of America, Inc.)

Ferdinand Porsche had an unconventional way of looking at things from the time he was a teenager in Maffersdorf, Northern Bohemia, in the old Austro-Hungarian Empire. He was born there September 3, 1875, in the golden glow of beloved Franz Josef's reign, into a world that seemed to run on slices of Sacher torte and hearty Viennese coffee with dollops of rich *schlag Sahne* on top, and which turned to

A Mercedes-Volkswagen? By the early 1920s Porsche dreamed of a good, small car accessible to the average man. He started to develop his concepts of a "people's car" based on an air-cooled rear engine, with swing-axle, torsion-bar suspension while he was technical director at Daimler-Benz in the mid-1920s. Such a car, the 130 and 170H, was actually produced by Mercedes-Benz in 1933–34, but the company preferred more conventional designs. Note the three-pointed star, without its circle, on the hood. (Courtesy Mercedes-Benz of America, Inc.)

an air-cooling system similar to his own), a sleek sports car that won Prince Henry's Prize in 1909 and earned a special silver plaque for its flawless performance, a tiny 1.1-liter Sascha sports car that won the rugged Sicilian Targa Floria race in 1922, and the aristocratic and revered Mercedes-Benz supercharged sports cars of the 1920s. In fact, it would be impossible to point to better or more varied automotive ancestors than the cars of Herbie's creator, Dr. Ferdinand Porsche, Europe's most innovative and respected automobile designer. Yet Herbie was, to say the least, a funny-looking kid and a little sickly there at the beginning. His father had deep pride and high hopes for him, but for a long time most people tended to think of little Herbie as the black sheep of an otherwise illustrious family.

Soon after Dr. Porsche opened his consulting firm in Stuttgart in 1930 he had corporate customers interested in his ideas about small cars. His first small-car project was for the Zundapp Motorcycle Company, which wanted changes in Porsche's basic concepts. This Zundapp prototype (one of three) used a twenty-six horsepower, five-cylinder, water-cooled rear engine but kept the aerodynamic fastback Beetle shape created by Porsche. (Volkswagen of America, Inc.)

the tune of Strauss waltzes. The glitter of Vienna didn't attract Ferdinand, a metalsmith's son apprenticed in his father's shop at fifteen, but the glitter of the first electric lights in Ginzkey's carpet mill in Maffersdorf fascinated him. He studied the system and before his seventeenth birthday built one for his father's shop. In the process he encountered something equally fascinating: the mill owner's new Daimler motorcar. Electricity and cars became his twin passions and he educated himself to get a job at an electrical company in Vienna. There he took classes at the technical college and sneaked

into the elite university lecture halls whenever he could get away with it.

Turn-of-the-century Vienna rivaled Paris and London for gaiety, prosperity, and general *joie de vivre,* and the newest way of demonstrating all three was by owning or at least being seen in a faddish new automobile. Ludwig Lohner, the Viennese coach builder who held the royal warrant from the emperor, saw an opportunity and tried to fill it with quiet, odorless electric cars. Lohner got in a bit over his head and turned to Porsche's employer for advice. Some

The NSU company retained Porsche in 1932 to develop his plan for an inexpensive small car. Work for NSU became known as the Type 32. One of the three prototypes, looking very Beetlelike, is shown outside Porsche's design office at 24 Kronenstrasse in Stuttgart.
(Volkswagen of America, Inc.)

of it came—uninvited—from young Porsche; and soon afterward he found himself working for Lohner with the dream assignment of designing a car—one which was run by electricity!

Porsche reasoned that in an automobile the source of power should be as near the point of its use as possible, a principle he retained throughout his career. The point of use in an automobile is, of course, the driving wheels (either front or rear), and that is exactly where he put an electric motor—one in the *center* of each of the wheels of his front-wheel-drive car. It was a radical departure from what the masters in Germany and France were doing, and old Ludwig Lohner shook his head. He had his doubts, but he had even greater faith in his youthful new chief designer. The car was praised at the 1900 Paris World's Fair and the Paris Exhibition, customers appeared at Lohner's door,

and Porsche's daring to think against the current was vindicated. Without fully realizing it, Porsche had reached a milestone in his life, which would be spent as an automobile designer who heard a different tune and marched to a different drummer.

While Lohner was delighted with the front-wheel-drive electric car, Porsche saw its shortcomings—limited range (32 miles), heavy batteries, and low speed (9 mph)—and he set out to solve them. He sensed that the answer lay in a compromise between the three competing systems for automotive power, electricity, steam, and the internal combustion engine. So he married two systems by discarding the heavy batteries and powering the twin electric "hub motors" with a generator turned by a small Daimler internal combustion engine. The system worked like a charm. The range was limited only by the fuel tank, and without the weight of the batteries the speed shot up to the legal limit on the U.S. roads of three quarters of a century later— 55 mph! Porsche's *Mixt* car was a technical triumph and a commercial success, so much so that old Ludwig didn't know what to do with all his customers. Porsche's credibility as a designer was solidly established, and just at that moment, he was drafted into the Austro-Hungarian army. His duty was hardly arduous, chauffering his own creation for the Archduke Franz Ferdinand, the man whose later assassination sparked World War I.

Porsche became a civilian again in 1905 and shortly afterward won the Poetting Prize, sort of the Austrian Oscar for auto design. Since Lohner wanted only to concentrate on production and sales, and Porsche wanted to create, he accepted the position of technical director at Austro-Daimler (*Oesterreicher-Daimler Motoren Werke*), the country's largest motor builders and constructors of Daimler's Mercedes *motorwagens* in Austria. Porsche's prestige may be measured by the fact that the position had recently been vacated by Daimler's son Paul. He took over with the full authority that his title implied and even ordered glass skylights

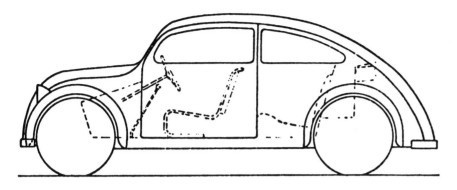

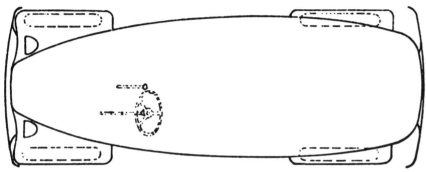

After Hitler began to exploit the small-car concept for political purposes the Volkswagen began to move. Dr. Porsche's proposal was formally set out in a document titled "Exposé concerning the construction of a German people's car"; accompanying it were drawings instantly familiar almost anywhere on earth half a century later.
(Volkswagen of America, Inc.)

Emil Jellinek offered to buy a year's production of Daimler's new model sports car of 1900 if it would be named for his daughter Mercedes. The deal was done, but the other half of his famous story is that Jellinek had another daughter, Maja, and the Austrian version of the car was named for her. Much of the Mercedes fame had been built by racing successes, and so Porsche followed the example and turned his attention to a works-prepared competition version of the Maja, as well as an important design contribution to the Mercedes *Mixt*, a racer using his own design of internal combustion engine powering a generator to run the electric motors powering the wheels.

Porsche's car for the 1909 run for Prince Henry's prize had increased power and modern shaft rather than chain drive. The Prince Henry competition was more akin to a rally than a race; it began in Berlin and meandered through the

A 1935 drawing of the Volkswagen prototype engine. Porsche's concepts for this horizontally opposed, air-cooled, rear-mounted engine dated back at least ten years, and his idea was constantly being refined.
(Volkswagen of America, Inc.)

to be installed in order to improve working conditions. While reportedly authoritarian about getting a job done *his* way, he was also democratic, and raised the eyebrows of the aristocratic board members when he discussed ideas with the ordinary workmen of another social caste. If there was any resentment of Porsche's recognition that a mechanic might also be able to think, it did not prevent his becoming a member of the board and later director general.

The company's mainstay at this time was the *Maja*, a companion car of the parent company's Mercedes. It had gotten its name when an Austro-Hungarian financier named

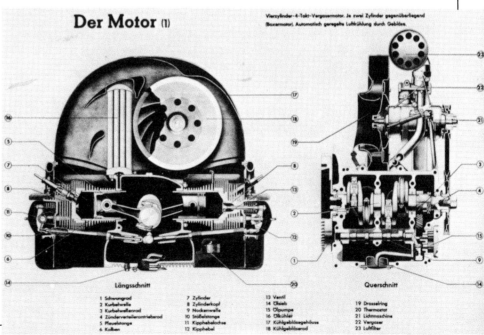

A 1936 "VW 3" as tested by the Society of German Automobile Manufacturers. Although the society saw the Volkswagen as state-financed competition, it tested three prototypes for thirty thousand miles, found them worthy of further development, and recommended thirty more test cars. (Volkswagen of America, Inc.)

Carpathian Mountains for a full week, to end in Budapest. Austro-Daimler entered three cars, each with driver and three passengers (Porsche's wife was one of his passengers), and each of the cars finished the event without one penalty point and were awarded a special silver plaque to commemorate the event. It is an interesting footnote to history that one of the test driver-mechanics working on Porsche's competition cars was a young man named Josip Broz who would become better known to the world as Tito of Yugoslavia.

Europe was emerging from its "hundred years of peace" and was again succumbing to the lure of marches, brass buttons, and nationalism. Porsche's talents were pressed into service as a designer of lightweight aircraft engines (which allowed him to develop his ideas about air cooling for internal combustion engines), and it was left to him to find a way to motorize a twenty-six-ton artillery piece. The war changed

Europe and the world; even Porsche the pure technician who dwelt in an abstract realm of calculus, tensile strengths, and coefficients of expansion saw that the changes, both technical and social, would profoundly affect his profession.

Aristocratic privilege was crumbling and Europe was poorer, yet middle-class expectations were rising and there was a cautious optimism that things might just get better, perhaps even on the American pattern which loomed as a pinnacle of prosperity in postwar Europe. The automobile was one of the chief symbols of aristocratic smugness; the cars Porsche had designed for Ludwig Lohner cost more than a fine house, and yet were rich men's toys. Even in America the car was sometimes seen as a sign of excess. Woodrow Wilson once said: "Nothing has spread socialistic feeling in this country more than the use of the automobile." The American President saw the motor car as "a picture of the arrogance of wealth with all its independence and carelessness." The fact that Henry Ford was turning the mass-produced automobile into a symbol of American democracy second only to the bald eagle seemed to escape Mr. Wilson. It did not, however, escape Ferdinand Porsche.

Porsche knew that advancing technology made possible smaller, cheaper cars that were as fast and reliable as bigger and more expensive cars. The Italian artist-engineer Ettore Bugatti had pioneered small, fast, and elite sports cars between one and two liters in displacement. These were also playthings of the rich (or at least the comfortably affluent), but Porsche saw a small, modestly priced automobile for the masses as a readily reachable reality. And as early as 1921 he proposed the idea of what would eventually become the Volkswagen to Austro-Daimler.

The board of directors could hardly dismiss an idea of their eminent *Herr Doktor* Porsche (honorary degree from Vienna Technical University, 1917) with a wave of the hand, but Porsche received no enthusiasm for a wild idea about "a people's car." The directors at Austro-Daimler in 1921—

indeed, the directors of virtually every automaker in Europe—were equally as hypnotized by the profits, prestige, and appeal of large cars as Detroit a half a century later. Porsche was a prophet without honor for the time being, and busied himself with designing the company's bread-and-butter big cars. Austro-Daimler did tolerate a single but spectacular small-car project, and that was a special sports car for Count Sascha Kolowrat, an Austrian movie mogul who wanted a small-displacement sports car for the rugged Targa Florio road race in Sicily. Porsche rose to the challenge with a pair of tiny but brilliant one-liter cars which were driven, not transported, to Sicily, finished first and second in the 1922 Targa Florio, and then driven home without a single breakdown. Porsche felt that he was at one of those times which "taken at the flood, leads on to fortune." He quickly developed a two-liter version of the Sascha sports car which hit 106 mph

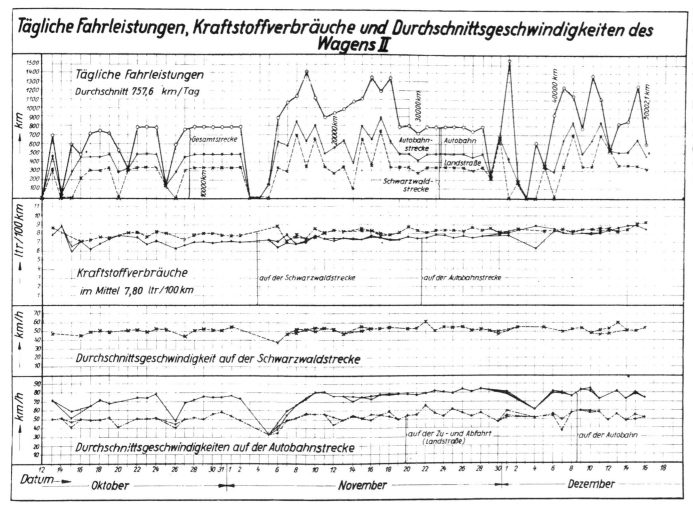

The Volkswagen was the most thoroughly tested automobile of its time. The graphs are a test driver's score sheet for test runs of the prototype VW 3 between October 12 and December 16, 1936, showing mileage, fuel consumption, and speed over the open road (*Autobahn*) and country roads (*Schwarzwald*, or Black Forest).
(Volkswagen of America, Inc.)

A comparison of the VW 3 (1936) on the right and the VW 30 (1937) on the left. (Volkswagen of America, Inc.)

and from which a small passenger car could be developed. He had his talking piece, but Austro-Daimler wasn't listening.

In has been said that Porsche quit Austro-Daimler because of the difference of opinion over small cars. Although it likely contributed, the reasons for Porsche's departure were more corporate than creative. For a time he relaxed at his villa on Lake Constance, cruised the lake in his motor yacht, and worked on a development of the small-car concept in his wine cellar. His hiatus ended when he accepted the position of technical director of *Daimler Motoren Gesellschaft* at Stuttgart, for the second time in his career replacing Paul Daimler.

Daimler's emphasis, like Austro-Daimler's, was big cars, and one of Porsche's projects was the development of a prewar Paul Daimler design for a *Hoechsleistung Tourenwagen*, or high-performance touring car. The 7.2-liter giant was far from Porsche's plans for a small car, but on the back burner at Stuttgart was a project that fascinated Porsche—a contrary and unobliging little 2-liter supercharged sports car. After Porsche laid hands upon it the temperamental machine responded by winning twenty-one of the twenty-seven races in which it was entered. That Porsche did much the same with the large-displacement supercharged prestige Mercedes and Mercedes-Benz sports cars of the 1920s is of course history. What is less-known history is that it was from Daimler-Benz (the result of a 1926 merger between the previously separate Daimler and Benz companies) that the world got its first look at an unusual, beetle-shaped little car with a

(Volkswagen of America, Inc.)

Thirty test cars called the VW 30 were built and tested in 1937, and the Beetle's bugs were swatted one by one. A Corporation for the Development of the Volkswagen was formed in 1937 with Dr. Porsche as a general manager, and he traveled to the U.S. to purchase tooling for the plant.

1.3-liter air-cooled horizontally opposed rear-engine car with a swinging rear axle. The concept—and silhouette—are so familiar that the Type 130 (and its larger-engined brother, the 170 H) would instantly be recognized today on any road in the world as a Volkswagen, except for the Mercedes-Benz three-pointed star on its beetle hood.

The rear axles of the 130 and 170 H (H = *Heckmotor*, rear engine) may well have owed credits to Daimler-Benz's suspension expert, Dr. Hans Nibel, but the rest of the little car was pure Porsche: engine over the rear wheels where the power was needed, aerodynamic body for reduced wind resistance, air cooling for simplicity and efficiency, a self-sure indifference to convention, and an overall uncomplicated machine suitable for mass production at under two thousand dollars (although still a high price in 1928 Germany).

So was the first Beetle really a Mercedes-Benz? In essence, yes; but Porsche's employer hardly saw the homely little machine as a mover and shaker of the industry. The 130 and 170 H were first produced in 1933 and 1934, and the company did have a real interest in a comparatively inexpensive bottom-of-the-line car. But the departure was too radical, and the emphasis soon shifted back to a front-engine, rear-drive, water-cooled 1.7-liter car of conventional design and appearance which, with variations, continued into the 1950s.

Porsche might be described as the classic round peg in a square hole at Daimler-Benz. Never the "compleat corporate animal," he felt restricted in the formal atmosphere and eschewed the corporate politics and intrigues. And he missed his native Austria. After an extremely fruitful five years at Stuttgart, Porsche went home to Austria in October 1928. At the beginning of 1929 he took the post of chief engineer of the Steyr works in Vienna, a "vertical industry" that produced everything from automobiles to automatic pistols. But, as Thomas Wolfe observes, you can't go home; a year and a half later corporate machinations again had Porsche at liberty.

This time he had had enough of corporations, and Porsche decided to start his own free-lance consulting firm specializing in automotive design. He returned to the "German Detroit" of Stuttgart and on December 1, 1930, opened his doors at 24 Kronenstrasse on what was to become a sort of automotive Bauhaus.

Porsche's first private client was the producers of the Wanderer automobile, and he designed and built prototypes of two cars for the company which would soon be absorbed into the Auto-Union combine and, three decades later, by Volkswagen itself. One of the Wanderer prototypes was a fastback coupé that exhibited the familiar Beetle shape except for its conventional front-engine compartment. Evidentally Porsche liked the look of the car and kept one of the prototypes for his personal use.

The Porsche Bureau on Kronenstrasse struggled financially, but enough customers came to the door to keep things moving. One day he opened the door to find several Russians standing there. In his career Porsche had been chief engineer and technical director for various companies, but the Russians' purpose in substance was to offer him the same authority for a whole country. As the guest of the Russian government on a grand tour for a month, Porsche was given a close-up of Russian industrialization the like of which no nation's secret service has seen. If Porsche's customers did not always realize what they were getting—one of Europe's most fertile mechanical minds—the Russians did, and they offered him *carte blanche*. The offer was tempting, but the price was high—a complete abandonment of Western Europe—and Porsche calculated that he couldn't afford it. It is interesting to pause for a moment to consider what his decision, made at a time of unsettled personal finances and political instability in Germany, meant to both East and West.

Another caller at Kronenstrasse was Dr. Fritz Neumeyer, proprietor of the Zundapp Motor Cycle Works. He had come to discuss a matter close to Porsche's heart, an effort

Dr. Ferdinand Porsche. (Volkswagen of America, Inc.)

old-line NSU company, picked up where Zundapp left off and in late 1932 gave Porsche a contract to develop his own original small car and to build three prototype models. For this car Porsche reverted to air cooling and designed a 1.5-liter, four-cylinder, horizontally opposed engine which was substantially the classic Volkswagen power plant. With all his groundwork on his original small-car plans behind him, Porsche made rapid strides with the car for NSU. Extensive tests proved the soundness of Porsche's ideas, and the car was fast (72 mph), agile, and could be produced more cheaply than any other car in Europe. But the air-cooled engine was noisy, and NSU's managing director, von Falkenhayn, described it as "sounding like a worn-out stone crusher." With more development Porsche was convinced that he had his "people's car" at last. But once again the "corporation men" would thwart him. Reinterpretation of a contract between NSU and Italy's Fiat was now seen to legally prevent independent NSU auto production, and Porsche's car became a casualty of a forgotten German corporation lawyer. Porsche then set aside the star-crossed small-car Project 12 and busied himself with designing great modernistic rear-engined Grand Prix cars for Auto-Union, even journeying to Long Island, New York, to watch his supercars win the Vanderbilt Cup race. But even there small cars filled his thoughts, and he made a trip to Michigan to see firsthand how Americans mass-produced cheap cars.

The NSU version of Project 12 represented original small-car technology at its height, all other small cars being merely scaled-down versions of conventionally designed larger cars. Yet, despite his creative thinking, Porsche had struck out with Austro-Daimler, Steyr, Daimler-Benz, Zundapp, and now NSU in his quest for a "people's car." There was often interest, sometimes enthusiasm, but in the end it always seemed that no one really wanted a good, cheap car— except the people who would buy and drive them. And for Porsche, now a struggling consultant, to become a manufacturer

which at the Porsche Bureau had become known as Project 12. Largely at his own expense, Porsche had poured all his pride, passion, and expertise into Project 12, a real "people's car." Neumeyer basically liked what he saw, but he wanted changes—a five-cylinder water-cooled engine instead of Porsche's three-cylinder noisy air-cooled design. In hopes of getting a "people's car" of some kind going at last. Porsche agreed. Three prototypes were built by 1932, but in that chaotic year in German history *Herr Doktor* Neumeyer got cold feet and cancelled the project.

Another, more adventuresome German entrepreneur, the

The 1936 VW prototype (right) and the 1937 (left). (Volkswagen of America, Inc.)

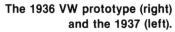

Prototype VW 30 (left) versus production model VW 38 (below). The visible changes were the welcome addition of a rear window, headlights flush with the front fenders, an enlarged hood lid, and safer front-hinged doors. The shape that would appeal, conquer, and endure had finally been reached. (Volkswagen of America, Inc.)

of a mass-produced car requiring millions in investment was out of the question. What Porsche needed was a powerful catalyst to interact between him and his market. Unknown to Porsche, one of history's most powerful reagents was then lurking in the shadows with a plot to do exactly that.

The marriage of Adolf Hitler and Volkswagen was a most unlikely alliance and one which, as we shall see, was never really consummated. Historians record Hitler as a devout car fancier, and the Hollywood image of him tearing along the Autobahn in a big, black, open Mercedes with supercharger screaming is largely correct. But what is less known is that Hitler never held title to a car in his own name, and never learned to drive. The fascination with powerful cars is understandable, but his inability to drive them—when considered with his reputed impotency—is food for interesting psychological postmortems. The idea of an underpowered, ugly little car with the power source in the "wrong" end could be expected to turn him off.

Hitler's introduction to motorcars in general and Mercedes in particular came through the sheerest chance: In the 1920s his insignificant political party had a small office in the same building in Munich where a businessman named Jacob Werlin had a Mercedes agency on the ground floor. The ancient association of politician and businessman was formed, and Hitler even became a customer—with party funds —in 1923. From then on Werlin was Hitler's unofficial counsel on all things automotive.

Whatever else it may be a symbol of, the automobile was a potent symbol of prosperity, and Hitler recognized that the *expectation* of owning a car was a powerful political lever to be manipulated as he wished. He intimated as much at the 1933 Berlin Auto Show only a few months after he became chancellor, and he hinted at a car accessible to the people, and would later cite the magnetic American example of a car in every garage. It was literally a generic description of Porsche's *Kleinauto*.

Hitler's pitch for the Volkswagen was almost pure California late show, used-car salesman; the equivalent of "A beautiful car at the impossible price of 990 marks! No cash down, credit for everybody! See Honest Adolf today! Hurry! Hurry! Hurry!" (Volkswagen of America, Inc.)

If Hitler was to be the catalyst for Porsche's "people's car," then Jacob Werlin was the obvious catalyst between Porsche and Hitler. As a member of the Daimler-Benz board of directors, Werlin knew Porsche and his work. In the fall of 1933 he asked Porsche to meet him at the Kaiserhof Hotel in Berlin. Porsche wondered why, but he obliged. When he arrived, Werlin dropped the shoe that Hitler was on the way over to talk to him about government production of a small car. Hitler described virtually the exact car Porsche had designed, and then dropped the other shoe when he priced the car at an absurd one thousand reichsmarks (about four hundred dollars).

We see almost daily proof that politicians have notoriously little regard for the cost of projects they propose "for the people." As a pragmatist, Porsche calculated the minimal price for the most basic "people's car" or *Volkswagen* at 1,550 marks, but Hitler the merchandiser of dreams wanted to promise a car—like any other automobile salesman—for "under 1,000 marks." Porsche the analyst thought it impossible, mad. Hitler the politician thought it merely a matter of "administration." Guess who won.

Porsche formally set down his proposal in a document titled "Exposé concerning the construction of a German people's car." Accompanying it were drawings instantly familiar almost anywhere on earth half a century later. Virtually from this point forward the Volkswagen was developed, tested, and financed as no car company in the world could have done, simply because the Volkswagen was no longer a car but a political device, even though the project was nominally under the private auspices of the Society of German Automobile Manufacturers. Porsche's contract called for a prototype Volkswagen in ten months and paid him at the modest rate of eight thousand dollars per month. A pair of cars known as the Volkswagen Series III (a sedan and a convertible) was ready by February 1936, somewhat late because of engine overheating problems and the unperfected torsion bar suspension. These two and a third car were extensively tested for thirty thousand miles between October 10 and 22 by the society (which viewed Porsche suspiciously as a government-subsidized competitor). But the test was fair, there was little complaint about the Volkswagen's performance, and thirty more test cars were suggested.

The next series of thirty cars, called VW-30, was built at the Mercedes factory, and two hundred soldiers were assigned to drive them in shifts for a million and a half miles to probe for flaws and weak points. No new car design had ever been so thoroughly tested, and as the test continued the drivers found less and less to complain about. Dr. Porsche's Volkswagen was nearly at the end of its ten-year development stage, and the moment for Hitler's miracle of "administration" was at hand.

He responded in the classic manner in which most politicians usually accomplish "great works," by quietly taking with the left hand and flamboyantly giving with the right. A plant to produce Volkswagens in the numbers required by Hitler (eventually a million and a half a year was projected) was a vast undertaking involving millions of marks and the largest automobile plant in the world—one nearly a mile long. A company "for the development of the Volkswagen" was formed on May 28, 1937, and financed with fifty million marks from the coffers of the German Labor Front. The Front was headed by Robert Ley, a master organizer who had run the Autobahn construction and other German WPA-type projects and who headed the *Kraft durch Freude* (Strength through Joy) movement. The KdF was that organ of the Nazi party which acknowledged that there was more to life than rigid devotion to work, and organized such party-sponsored amenities (read propaganda devices) as cruises, holidays, operas, and concerts, and now even the perhaps possible dream of a Volkswagen.

Over the years the forward storage space would be substantially enlarged over the limited original "trunk" of the Model 38. The energy-absorbing qualities of the front-mounted spare are a safety feature. (Volkswagen of America, Inc.)

The heart of the matter. Porsche's concept of the horizontally opposed air-cooled, four-cylinder rear engine for a small car was revolutionary yet simple and eminently practical—a "Why didn't I think of that?" idea. The original was 27½ horsepower—noisy, but rugged and cheap to run. (Volkswagen of America, Inc.)

Austere dash panel of the VW Model 38. The majority of anticipated VW buyers had never driven, and Germany had the highest accident rate in Europe, so the large shift pattern in the dash was probably a good idea. (Volkswagen of America, Inc.)

A second batch of thirty cars was tested for fifty thousand miles apiece, and the final evolution of the Volkswagen with familiar flush headlights and full-length hood lid—the Type 38—was ready for production. Hitler now had tangible, shiny lacquered bait to dangle before his customers. His pitch was almost pure California late show used-car salesman: "A beautiful car at the impossible price of 990 marks! No cash down, credit for everybody! See Honest Adolf today! Hurry! Hurry! Hurry!" And, as with all con artists, it was what he didn't say that really mattered—250 marks extra for insurance and delivery charges (even though the car was to be picked up at the factory), and the fine print was a bit vague about delivery dates.

The "credit" was a slight variation on the "buy now, pay later" plan; it was more like "pay now, get later (maybe)." The price of 990 marks ($396) was a lot of money in Germany. It represented about 800 hours of work for the average German, and very few people had that much in cash. And, under Hitler's plan, it wouldn't have done a buyer much good even if he had the cash.

Volkswagen merchandising was innovative or inane, depending upon your viewpoint. As have myriad marketeers before and since, Robert Ley considered the question of how best to sell cars to people who really couldn't afford them. His answer was a sort of savings-stamp plan. Every week the butcher, baker, and munitions maker would march to his friendly neighborhood Nazi party office and buy a stamp for about two dollars. He pasted it in a book and when the book was filled he was entitled to (wait for) a Volkswagen. Simple—if you didn't think too much about it. A bit later the minimum payment was reduced to two dollars *a month*; even easier terms, if you didn't stop to calculate how long it would take to collect all the stamps. Even at that, perhaps Honest Adolf overestimated his customers; less than 337,000 in all took the bait, while he was gearing up for millions. But each of them also overestimated Der Führer; not a single Volkswagen was ever delivered to a stamp collector, and at the end of the war the millions of marks in the KdF account were in a bank located a few yards inside the Russian zone—and they stayed there.*

As tens of thousands of Germans started their stamp books and looked gleefully forward to weekend traffic jams in the Black Forest, the fat was in the fire and some sixty-odd demo Beetles (hand built at many times 990 marks apiece, incidentally) were soon going to wear thin. Delivery on Honest Adolf's dream machine presupposed an automobile factory of unheard-of proportions. This grand project was referred to the chief architect of the Third Reich, Albert Speer, who considered a mile-long automobile factory and attendant town beneath his talents while his attention was directed to redesigning Berlin on Hitlerian scale. He delegated this prosaic duty to the architecture department of the University of Brunswick, and the end result was the selection of an unknown young architect named Peter Koller, who brilliantly built not only a giant factory and a planned new town but the one notable architectural artifact of the era as well.

Aside from Koller's technical competence, much of the creation of the Volkswagen plant lay in a realm somewhere between Gilbert and Sullivan and Mel Brooks. The requirement of a lot of open land and reasonable accessibility eventually led the master planners to an inhospitable moor in Lower Saxony dotted with mosquito-infested swamps. From their scout plane, the only landmarks were the brooding fourteenth century Castle Wolfsburg of the proud Count Werner von der Schulenberg, a mound of earth called Klieversberg Hill, and the town of Fallersleben, a provincial place where the centuries merged into the mists drifting off the moor. A film director would have relished the spot as a perfect location for *Dracula Strikes Back*.

One day some official-looking Nazi types drove up and

suggested to the old count that his estate would make a fine gift to the Third Reich for a Volkswagen factory. The count and his ancestors had enjoyed unbroken title all the way back to 1135 when Emperor Lothair II had bestowed the land on a faithful knight. Throughout the next 802 years the most serious assault on the von der Schulenbergs came from the swamp mosquitos and pesky gnats, which most likely explains their uncontested possession, and raises some doubts about the true value of the services performed by their ancestory. However, be it ever so humble, there's no place like home, and the count was determined to hold onto every mosquito and cat-o'-nine-tails.

Despite his baronial life-style, the count was no medieval relic, and he was too sophisticated to think that frontal assaults on bureaucracies (especially totalitarian ones) ever work. He was Machiavellian enough to realize that the best way to wage war on a bureaucracy is to set it against itself. His plan of attack would gladden the hearts of modern environmentalists. He convinced the forestry service that the old oaks in the area were national treasures, and reminded them of Hitler's own save-a-tree program. And he alerted the Nazi equivalent of the Environmental Protection Agency that his ancestral insects were an endangered species. The Nazi EPA bit hard on that one and sent out an insect expert who went into entomological rapture over the place and its dozens of species of rare bugs which no one had ever bothered to catalog. His report was explicit that the area shouldn't be touched lest the breeding grounds be disturbed. The forestry people were similarly paternalistic about the oaks, and the count envisioned something like the later great American snafu over the snail darter at the Tellico Dam. But just to be sure, he dropped hints to old army friends on the General Staff that a mile-long factory directly on the Mittleland Canal would be quite a nice gift to the navigators of enemy bombers.

It was an excellent plan and under more ordinary

---

*Eventually, Volkswagen settled all such claims.

In 1940 the Volkswagen plant converted to production of the VW Type 82, the military VW nicknamed the *Kübelwagen*, or "bucket car." About fifty thousand were built between 1940 and 1945. Their waterless engines, springless suspension, and rear-engine traction endeared them to Rommel, the Desert Fox, and they proved just as valuable in Russian winters and mud. American G.I.'s established an exchange rate of two Jeeps for one *Kübelwagen*.

(Volkswagen of America, Inc.)

conditions would have tied the government in knots for years to come. But its weakness was that Nazi Germany was not a pure bureaucracy; it had an overlord whose temper tantrums could cut the thickest red tape. All of these factors came to Hitler's attention and, like Queen Victoria, he was not amused. One resists a scene set at Berchtesgaden or some like stage with Hitler storming, *"Nein, nein! We Nazis will not be defeated by gnats!"* Yet its equivalent was played out somewhere and the bulldozers advanced on Fallersleben like panzer divisions. Hitler laid the cornerstone for the VW factory on May 26, 1938, amid a full panoply of drum and bugle corps, uniforms, sixty-foot banners, bands, cheering crowds, and propaganda which praised the place as about the greatest construction project since the pyramids. Some seventy thousand people were there, and one of them was Ferdinand Porsche, and, as far as can be determined, now the titular head of Volkswagenwerke GmbH. He was aware that his beloved little car had fallen in with bad company, but one thing had sort of led to another. As Der Führer droned on, he mused that if one of the companies he had tried to convince about small cars had listened to him, it might not have come to this spectacle. His musings were abruptly halted when Hitler announced that in recognition of the efforts of the *Kraft durch Freude* organization to make the "people's car" a reality, it would forever be known as *Der KdF Wagen.* Those present who saw the car as hardware rather than propaganda suppressed an autonomic retch at the idea, and mentally wrote off any plans for ever exporting a vehicle ludicriously called "the strength-through-joy car." And among the engineers present who wondered at the wisdom of building a giant factory in a sandy swamp, there was the haunting suspicion of Hitler's swastika-incised cornerstone sinking slowly into the mire while mosquitos and gnats buzzed victoriously. None of this, of course, entered the principal speaker's thoughts as he climbed into a VW convertible to pose for photographers and drive back to his special train.

Ferdinand Porsche watched with the same suppressed sad expression often seen in his photographs as his son drove that convertible Volkswagen away from the ceremony and the top-hatted, white-clad masons washed down their tools from the ceremonial mortaring.

The Volkswagen plant was completed and it was a legitimate masterwork. However, it never produced a single Volkswagen for a private German citizen for nearly ten years. Before the factory was completed it was converted to military contracts, and 630 VWs were built and delivered to the government in 1940 before the plant was converted to production of the Type 82, a four-door reconnaisance vehicle which evolved as a rugged and versatile German Jeep. The *Kübelwagen* (literally "bucket car") was initially suspect by the military, but one officer who saw its potential was Erwin Rommel, better known as the Desert Fox. Rommel found the *Kübelwagen* ideal for the desert, and its value may be measured by the fact that a VW was invariably the last vehicle to be abandoned. Meanwhile, commanders on the frozen Russian front were making similar discoveries about the value of its spring-less suspension, waterless engine, and mud-defying traction. Later, Americans would be making the same discoveries and G.I.'s established the unofficial exchange rate of one *Kübelwagen* for two Jeeps. A fascinating variation on the *Kübelwagen* was the *Schwimmwagen,* an amphibious VW complete with propeller, snorkel for the engine and exhaust, and one of the most interesting accessories ever to come with a motor vehicle—a wooden paddle. At one point port and starboard red and green lights were considered.

The first Allied bombs fell on the Volkswagen plant in 1940 with little actual damage. The plant was not a prime target but, as Count von der Schulenberg had warned, it was an easy one, and the buzz of Allied engines often interrupted the hum of the turbines. For the workers, many of them foreign, it was a dangerous target; the swampland

A *Kübelwagen* with a history. This Type 82 left Wolfsburg early in 1943 for a fighter squadron's base in North Africa. It was returned to Germany near the end of the war and served on a farm from 1945 to 1947 and later as a utility vehicle for an automobile repair garage. From 1949 to 1966 it was used on hunting expeditions in northern Germany. For the next three years it was used as a passenger car by someone with either a limited budget or unusual tastes. In 1970 it was purchased by a U.S. Air Force officer who intended to bring it home and restore it to its 1943 appearance. It has appeared as an extra in various TV shows and films, including a part in *The Bridge at Remagen.* (Volkswagen of America, Inc.)

The Schwimmwagen was an amphibious VW complete with propeller and a snorkel for the engine—and a paddle. At one point port and starboard (red and green) marine lights were considered. The type 166 had four-wheel drive and a thirty horsepower 1131 cc engine. About fourteen thousand were built. (Volkswagen of America, Inc.)

construction site precluded underground bomb shelters. Besides *Kübelwagen*s and *Schwimmwagen*s the plant was cranking out everything from airplane wings and hand grenades to barracks stoves. Finally in April 1944, it got full attention when three flights of bombers hit it with incendiaries and high explosives. By the war's end about three quarters of Peter Koller's masterpiece lay in ruins.

With it lay Porsche's dream of a "people's car"; Porsche himself would spend nearly two of his last years in prison as victim of a bizarre plot to build a "French Volkswagen" and the combined opposition of both French communists and French capitalists. The plant itself was in the British zone of occupation, and in time the mechanics of Wolfsburg sought to repair British army vehicles in exchange for a few food rations. From this start the plant was established as an official repair depot for British vehicles. Transport of any kind was in short supply; the bombed and overextended

Most people boast over their VW's mpg; the driver of this one calculated in kilometers per cubic meter of propane. Even without OPEC there was a fuel shortage in Germany, and this Beetle was modified to ignore the benzine shortage. (Volkswagen of America, Inc.)

After the war the Wolfsburg plant was in the British zone and became a vehicle repair center under the command of the Royal Electrical and Mechanical Engineers. The British and VW personnel discovered that a few new cars could be assembled in the bombed factory for the depleted British motor pools. There were 713 such 1945 VWs built, some of the world's first postwar automobiles. This was one of them. (Volkswagen of America, Inc.)

A 1946 VW made for the British occupation forces, one of ten thousand built that year. The big change appears to have been the jazzy two-tone wheels. (Volkswagen of America, Inc.)

British auto industry was already at work on its desperately needed export market, and visions of Jaguars and MGs danced in their heads. So the occupation army in Germany was told to make do. Technicians of the Royal Electrical and Mechanical Engineers headquartered at the plant in Wolfsburg did so by discovering that there was enough undamaged or repairable equipment to build complete cars. The workers gleefully bent their backs to the task for a few occupation marks, and counted themselves lucky to be among the first workers in Germany to become reemployed. By the end of 1945 they had built 713 new Volkswagens. They were some of the world's very first postwar cars, and they came from a factory that nobody legally owned and nobody wanted.

3/Across the Wide Atlantic

One of the first commercial views of a Volkswagen that Americans saw in print was this 1949 piece of advertising literature which shows the 1949 Deluxe model. (Courtesy Terry Shuler, VVWCA)

Volkswagen's rapid rise to respectability and riches is the classic "orphan boy makes good," Horatio Alger, nose-to-the-grindstone story which is traditionally more New World than Old. If there is a single hero to the tale, it is a man named Heinz Nordhoff, whose original impression of the *Kinderwagen* was about as positive as the famous response from the chairman of the board of Ford Motor Company who, when offered the Volkswagen plant literally free in early 1948, replied that he didn't think it was "worth a damn." British and Australian automakers felt about the same, and the occupation power gladly turned the whole leaky, bombed-out, makeshift mess at Wolfsburg over to Nordhoff.

Actually, Nordhoff's opinion of the Volkswagen and that of Ford's big wheel had more common background and perspective than perhaps either of them realized. Nordhoff had been put in charge at Wolfsburg by the British occupation forces because of his prewar auto experience and accomplishment at Adam Opel AG—and because he was handy at the moment. Opel was a venerable German firm; it had been founded as a sewing machine factory at the time Americans were fighting the Battle of Gettysburg. One of the founder's sons, Fritz, became interested in the new *Motorwagen*, built a prototype car in 1898, and had four models on the market by 1902. By 1912 they were

Nordhoff came in the early 1930s. He absorbed and applied what he learned in both Germany and the U.S., and his ideas about automobiles—as well as his accent—became American by osmosis. His thoughts about the Volkswagen as it was being developed and promoted in the 1930s was that it was a political gimmick for Hitler rather than a real car—and that if it *was* a car it wasn't good for General Motors. Up until the day he inherited Wolfsburg by fate or fortune he had ridden only a few miles in a Volkswagen.

Exposure to the little car—and to the enthusiasm of the Wolfsburg workers for it—brought Nordhoff to the realization that the Volkswagen was not a joke but a car, and a

The earliest Beetles made their way across the Atlantic with returning U.S. servicemen, who were the first Americans to become infected with Beetlemania. (Krishman Photographic Service)

The Basic Beetle of 1948 was basic indeed; noisy, harshly sprung, devoid of chrome or the slightest ornament, even down to the absence of wheel covers. But it was hardy, dependable, and virtually unbreakable. (Volkswagen of America, Inc.)

building thirty-two hundred cars a year. Fritz Opel admired not only cars, but the way Americans built cars, and in 1923 he came to see firsthand the magic of Detroit. He became a staunch convert; seven years later an "affiliation" of the Russelheim factory with that synonym for American technique—General Motors—began. The venture gave GM access to the German market, and gave Opel access to to American production methods. It was into this most Americanized piece of the German auto industry that young

(Volkswagen of America, Inc.)

Willkomm zu Amerika—1949. The welcome was hardly warm. A Dutchman who was sent to introduce America to the wonders of the Beetle had to sell his sample Volkswagen to pay his hotel bill, and sailed back to Europe leaving a single, lonely "officially imported" Beetle in the U.S.

In 1949 we sold 2 Volkswagens in the U.S.A.

Volkswagen got off to a slow start in America, and was not ashamed to say so later in its ads. This pair of original immigrant 1949 Beetles multiplied like bunnies and by 1968, instead of two cars a year, Volkswagen was selling two cars every two and a half minutes in the U.S. (Volkswagen of America, Inc.)

car with a character and rationale all its own. And he came to recognize that fate had given him what no automobile executive ever had before: an automobile factory to run completely as he pleased, without a board of directors or stockholders—or anybody—to account to. The slate may have had a few bomb craters here and there, but it was otherwise clean.

Nordhoff applied the traditional German virtues of unrelenting hard work to his adopted American corporate philosophy. He lived at the factory—there wasn't any place else to live at the time—and he worked seven-day weeks, working practically all his waking hours. His workers worked hard too, but none too efficiently in a largely unheated, semi-operational factory. It took the nearly seven thousand workers a year to produce only six thousand cars, less than one car per man per year. Three months after Wolfsburg was dumped on Nordhoff, he received some extraordinary help. The new deutsche mark, at an official exchange rate of just over four to the dollar, was established, and Germany was set firmly on the free enterprise-capitalist highway with its motor running. From that point on Germany as a whole, with Marshall Plan assistance, moved forward to recovery and prosperity. The detailed blossoming of a wounded and unwanted war casualty into one of the brightest industrial successes in the world, itself a major impetus in Germany's *Wirtschaftwunder*, or economic miracle, under Nordhoff's hand is told at length in such histories as *Small Wonder* by Walter Henry Nelson (Little, Brown & Co., Boston), *Beyond Expectation* by K. B. Hopfinger (G. T. Foulis & Co., London), or *The VW Beetle* by Robin Fry (David & Charles, London).

The success of Volkswagen in a recovering Europe virtually devoid of consumer goods is one thing. How the same car could conquer the automotive world, put people on wheels who had never dreamed of a car of their own, and change the concepts and purchasing patterns of the greatest car-consuming country in the world is quite another.

Selling Volkswagens in the United States in the late 1940s was considerably more difficult than the old joke about selling refrigerators to Eskimos. After all, summer eventually comes even in the Yukon. However, there was precious little summer sunshine for Volkswagen in America in those early days. The Beetle was "foreign" in the U.S. from any angle. It was small, noisy, unconventional in apperance; if anything, it harked back to the simple days of "tin lizzies" which Americans were busy trying to bury under yards of chrome and acres of sculptured sheet metal. Americans were hungry

The 1952 Volkswagen offered such niceties as windows that cranked up and down with three and a half turns of the handle; it had previously required ten and a half revolutions. Hedonistic decadence was setting in early. (Volkswagen of America, Inc.)

The '52 Beetle also heralded the introduction of vent windows for improved ventilation. Twenty years later other makers were heralding their absence as progress rather than a production shortcut. (Volkswagen of America, Inc.)

for new cars, but not *that* hungry—or so it seemed. And the Beetle had the stigma of being "Hitler's car" at a time when the war was hardly ancient history.

Volkswagen did not try to crack the formidable American market in those days just to sell cars. Its order books were comfortably plump; almost from the beginning of Nordhoff's tenancy Volkswagen had no difficulty in selling cars in Europe and elsewhere. Soon its difficulties were in building as many cars as it could sell. And thereby lay the attraction of the American market. Nordhoff needed new American equipment to keep up with the increasing demand for cars, and that meant he needed American dollars to pay for it. Now, in those days, before double-digit inflation and fast printing presses at the Bureau of Printing and Engraving, the eagle on the greenback was a rare bird and hard to snare.

The best way to import something from America (providing that its government wasn't giving it to you) was to sell something to Americans for their hard currency. Heinz Nordhoff needed industrial equipment and he had Volkswagens.

Nordhoff felt that the VW could stand on its own four wheels as a good car if given a fair chance. To help counter the sticky PR problem arising from the Beetle's Hitler-era origins, he sent the first official Volkswagen not with a German but with a Dutchman on Holland-America Lines' *Westerdam* to New York. The man was Ben Pon, armed with a single Volkswagen and some spare parts. He had established one of Volkswagen's first export markets in neighboring Holland, overcoming staunch Dutch hostility to anything even remotely German. Nordoff hoped the silver-tongued Heer Pon could do as well with the Americans. He didn't. Pon

For 1953 emphasis continued on those vent windows; their handles now had a locking button to keep them put where placed. The big visible change was the abandonment of the vintage split rear windows, previously the mark of the rugged individualist and true pioneer among American owners. (Volkswagen of America, Inc.)

Gott in Himmel! Ist das ein Beetle? Directional signals on the front fenders replace the quaint and very European side-mounted semaphores, and a *sunroof* becomes available for 1955. A mini-limo, no less.
(Volkswagen of America, Inc.)

On October 27, 1955, Volkswagen of America was incorporated and promptly bought a plant in New Jersey to manufacture Beetles like this 1955 model with "plumber's delight" bumper guards. The plan was dropped when it was discovered that the cost of duplicating VW quality standards in as-yet-undevalued 1955 dollars was prohibitively expensive.
(Volkswagen of America, Inc.)

1958 was the first year for the enlarged, non-oval rear window and larger windshield in all models. The "home market" model shown retains the side semaphore directional signals and small bumpers. (Volkswagen of America, Inc.)

The 1959 export model was a duplicate of the 1958. *Plus ça change, plus c'est la même chose.* (Volkswagen of America, Inc.)

Into the Super Sixties. Big changes for 1960 were a push-button door handle and the beginnings of safety features like a recessed steering wheel, padded visors, and an anti-sway bar for more control. Comfort increased, too, with contoured seats and a footrest for the front seat passenger. (Volkswagen of America, Inc.)

The millionth Volkswagen was built in 1955; by 1962 the millionth VW to be shipped to America arrived, and by 1965 the ten millionth VW was built. The Volkswagen plants of the sixties were replacing the image of Henry Ford as the master of mass production. They could roll out over five thousand VWs a day. (Volkswagen of America, Inc.)

and Beetle were welcomed as if they were carrying bubonic plague, hoof-and-mouth disease, and the common cold. In less than a month Pon had run out of money, had to to sell the car and spares for eight hundred dollars to pay his hotel bill, and retreated across the Atlantic. An inauspicious beginning.

A few months later Nordhoff tried again, and sold another Beetle. The pair was immortalized years later in a Volkswagen ad under the obtuse boast, "In 1949 we sold two Volkswagens in the U.S.A." Actually, Volkswagen could have ignored the American market forever and prospered, but it didn't. The company persevered: Each single sale was a small victory. The next year a whopping 330 were sold. One by one, dealers who found a ready market for Jaguars, MGs, and, ironically, Porsches began to look at the very unsporty (but cheap) Beetle. A few ordered samples, and to their surprise and pleasure found that their clients who paused to look a little longer and liked what they found, liked it a lot. Curiously, as you got past distributors and dealers and down to the paying customers, Volkswagens got easier to sell—at least to certain people. And converts, always the most zealous in their newfound faith, tend to proselytize. American customers and dealers alike were getting their first exposure to the *mystique* of the homely little beast, which would later be explained in terms of Jungian psychic symbology, mystic or occult attraction, or simply in pragmatic terms that it did what a car is supposed to do very well indeed—and nothing else.

And then there was Volkswagen's "secret weapon"— service. The sleekest and sexiest "furrin" sports cars, with their twin cams and prima donna temperaments, soon bogged down for lack of spare parts and knowledgeable mechanics who didn't greet you with, "What kind of car is *that*?" For the tiny number of Beetles in the U.S. by 1953 (just over twenty-five hundred export models plus whatever U.S. servicemen brought home with them), Volkswagen spent a disproportionate amount of time and money seeing that they

The horsepower race rages on. In 1954 engine size was raised from 1131 cc to 1192 cc, and horsepower went up from 30 to 36, and up to 40 HP in 1961. For 1966 displacement was escalated to 1300 cc and horsepower was up to 50. A regular muscle car. (Volkswagen of America, Inc.)

Power begets power. In 1967 displacement moved up to 1.5 liters and horsepower to 53. Detroit was distraught by this newest power provocation, but more so by the fact that in that year VW sold 443,510 vehicles of all types in the U.S. (Volkswagen of America, Inc.)

1968: the "plumber's delight" bumpers go and headrests on the front seats come. Progress will just not be stilled. The hood accessory was strictly optional. (Volkswagen of America, Inc.)

kept chuffing along with the least amount of bother to their owners. Teams of teaching mechanics drove around the country to instruct in the strange but simple skills needed to keep the Beetle happy in harness, and parts seemed to be at hand when needed—which was a very great deal more than could be said for other imported cars. Word got around that it might be ugly, noisy, and stiffly sprung, but it was cheap, it worked, and you could keep it working.

Even at that, America lagged well behind the rest of the world, which was rapidly becoming accustomed to a stiff standard of service from exclusive Volkswagen dealerships operated according to strict rules set in Wolfsburg—even down to what the showroom and shop should be like and the

cut and color of mechanics' uniforms, and their cleanliness. It was the German penchant for order and orderliness given full reign.

All of this changed as Volkswagen continued to grow in the U.S., admittedly Topsy-like for a time, until there was enough grass-roots strength to warrant the founding of Volkswagen of America, Inc., on October 27, 1955, a subsidiary corporation of the parent company in Germany. This corporation now coordinated importation, distribution, sales, and standards for Volkswagen service in the United States. America had finally become a full-fledged member of the "Volkswagen family of nations." Volkswagen's American ambitions were high, very high for 1955. It is seldom remembered

It was inevitable: a Beetle that could shift for itself. In 1969 VW introduced the automatic stick shift, a sort of clutchless automatic that let you stick it in drive or go through the gears, whichever suited your mood. Neat, but purists nearly died.
(Volkswagen of America, Inc.)

1970. Both the 57 HP engine and the taillights got bigger. Sales did not.
(Volkswagen of America, Inc.)

By 1971 emission controls on U.S. models were biting into the Beetle's ability to deal with the 1970s, and horsepower had to rise to cope with the "inefficiency factors" which emission standards meant for all cars. And, shades of Cadillac, there was now a memory switch to turn off the headlights when you switched off the ignition. Ferdinand Porsche's ghost must have turned a somersault. (Volkswagen of America, Inc.)

On the twenty-seventh of August, 1971, Volkswagen shipped its five millionth car to the United States, and celebrated with the Super Beetle—the ultimate Bug. Proud, imperious, and menacing, the Super Beetle was a full three inches longer than its little brother, and was powered by a 60 HP engine, double the power of the original car. (Volkswagen of America, Inc.)

The 1974 Super Beetle was meeting U.S. safety regulations with energy-absorbing bumpers and a self-centering steering system to prevent skidding on slippery surfaces. Beetles were guaranteed for twelve months or twenty thousand miles. (Volkswagen of America, Inc.)

This 1975 Beetle was one of the eighteen million that had been produced by that year. Japanese and American competition—plus higher U.S. prices because of dollar devaluation—was being felt, and Volkswagen was calling the Beetle "the benchmark by which other small cars are judged." (Volkswagen of America, Inc.)

that in the year of its founding Volkswagen of America, Inc., bought a plant in New Jersey for the assembly of American Beetles, the first time anybody had thought about building a foreign car in the U.S. since Rolls-Royce gave up the Silver Ghost assembly plant in Springfield, Massachusetts, in the early 1930s. The plan was dropped as the estimates to maintain VW-quality standards accelerated beyond import costs, but it was indicative of how the company saw the American market and how early.

America's interest in Beetles, seemingly only spurred on by the endless jokes and derision of the yet unenlightened, progressed almost geometrically. The real explosion would come when Volkswagen started telling people about its cars in ads as radical and ahead of their time as the car itself. But by that time Beetles had not only crossed the wide Atlantic and landed, but were chewing their way to Detroit, and on to legend. How American the funny-looking little foreigners became is best remembered by the quote from a Midwest housewife who said (in a Volkswagen ad), "I don't want an imported car; I want a Volkswagen."

Under the engine lid, fuel injection; outside, metallic paint and sports-type wheels; inside, velour upholstery. Together, La Grande Bug for 1975. (Volkswagen of America, Inc.)

Why so many Volkswagens live to be 100,000.

kswagen isn't the kind of a car you
fter a year or two.
igned and built for keeps.
tan speed in a Volkswagen is slower
n many other cars. That means less
gine friction and stress are so low
W's cruising speed is the same as

Continuity in making the same basic model
year after year has led to Volkswagen's qual-
ity of assembly—the kind that a $5,000 car
would be proud of; to say nothing of a car
that sells for $1,585.*

Just to give you an idea: A Volkswagen is
so airtight, it's a good practice to open the
window before you slam the door. Even after

you've had it for several years.
So. If you own a '61 or '62 VW that you'
taken good care of, why would you want
trade it in for a '66—which looks just like it?
You wouldn't.
You'd keep it, and have t
pleasure of seeing 99,999 on yo
VW's odometer turn to xxxxx

4/The Ads

If you ask ten people to recall a good magazine ad or TV commercial, probably nine of them can't do it without using the word *Volkswagen* in their first dozen words.

If the Beetle is one of the most successful cars ever built (and that's a hard argument to lose), then the advertising campaign waged to win the hearts and minds and checkbooks of prospective customers—as well as to assure VW owners that they made the correct decision—was one of the ad business's crown jewels. It was, of course, the softest of the soft sells. Volkswagen ads never told you that you couldn't live without a Beetle, although they determinedly suggested you could live a bit more economically with one. They never used words like *longer, lower, wider, best, chic, beautiful,* etc. In fact, they hardly ever used adjectives at all, and when they did they used ones strictly verboten in the automobile business: words like *ugly, lemon,* and *ugh.* They carried self-deprecation to the point of paying to print pictures like one of a Beetle with a flat tire and of another being hauled away behind a tow truck. The caption under the latter picture read, "A thing like this could happen, even to a Volkswagen. After all, it's only human." An adman suggesting that Ford or GM actually buy magazine space or air time to show its product in a compromising position of less than surreal perfection and prestige would have been not so gently shoved in the direction of the unemployment office. Naturally, the result was that the sheer refreshment value of Volkswagen ads made people notice them, enjoy them, laugh at them, remember them, talk about them, look for them, and even read them. When they finally made TV, people actually called local stations and asked when such and such an ad was scheduled or if it could be rerun so Aunt Edna could see it. Do you remember the last time you called a TV station to ask for a rerun of your favorite deodorant commercial?

To appreciate what advertising did for Volkswagen—and what Volkswagen did for advertising—it is necessary to recollect what auto ads were like in the year One B. B. (Before Beetles). A perusal of magazines of the era of the middle and late 1950s is not unlike looking at Gay Nineties' newspaper ads of the sort reproduced on laminated plastic tabletops at Wendy's "old-fashioned" hamburger emporiums. In comparison to the Volkswagen ads that followed they are just that quaint and dated. From the perspective of the eighties (which are not shaping up as exactly the high-water mark of the American auto industry), the only conclusion to be drawn from those ads is that people were either pretty hard up for wheels, or they bought the cars in spite of the advertising. From the pages of the April 1956 *National Geographic* glows a charcoal and pink Pontiac (remember *that* combination?) with a cute little pair of watercolor people peering through the windshield. The headline reads: "America's Best Dressed Car Puts

On Its Running Shoes!"—"Try This One for Sighs!" (!!!) Lincoln was running a painting of a Premier elongated on the drawing board and posed next to a cretin-sized couple to emphasize the caption, "Never before a Lincoln so long . . . and so longed for." Chrysler was touting "The Year Ahead Car" in those days. Ford was telling you, "They're not making the hills as high this year." Their emphasis was on V-8 power ("You'll pass in a split jiffy.") and Thunderbird styling ("Here's styling that will stay in style."). Presumably, at least until September.

Before Volkswagen, American auto advertising was very standardized, and very sterile. (An opinion: Much of it still is.) It would have been possible to slip in a picture of a competitor's car, regardless of price or rank, and use the same copy by changing only the name. Photographs of cars were fairly unusual in Detroit ads of the day; drawings left great latitude to the artist's brush to make the machine appear as the King Kong of motordom. Big, of course, meant good. Even the best camera wizards of Germany and Japan couldn't devise a lens that would simultaneously enlarge the car and shrink the admiring courtiers around it. When photographs and real people were used, the people had to look like surrogates of Vanderbilt and Rockefeller ilk and the car had to appear as a principal part of their anointment as arbiters of the good life. Above all, the ads projected a reverence for the car. It was an object of worship, and those permitted in its presence (i.e., by purchase) became cohabitors of Olympus.

It was into this wonderful and slightly wacky world of selling the Detroit machine and its attendant psychology that the Beetle came to compete for attention in print and, later, film. To say the least it was a test of courage and judgment— and of luck. As fate had it, the Beetle people had all three, but few conventional admen would have been willing to bet a bent bumper on that when Volkswagen first made the decision to advertise.

Doyle Dane Bernbach did what few agencies bother to do: They got to know their product intimately. A team went to Wolfsburg to see the birthing of a Beetle, from raw steel to final shipment. From their involvement came honest ads for an honest car, like "After we paint the car we paint the paint," and "It takes this many men to inspect this many Volkswagens" (hundreds of white-coated inspectors behind one Beetle). The ads made the point that quality *could* come from an assembly line. (Volkswagen of America, Inc.)

That decision did not come easily. By the late 1950s Volkswagen was a formidable *fait accompli* at home, in the U.S., and elsewhere. By 1955 the millionth Beetle had been built, at a rate of a thousand a day, and it was not nearly enough. Wolfsburg, and later other sites, were cranking out VWs on multiple shifts, but the supply never seemed to quite equal the demand. Even after Nordhoff invested $125 million in earnings in 1959 to boost production to three thousand cars a day, there were still back orders and waiting customers. A similar amount was again invested almost immediately in expanding facilities, and by the end of 1960 the flow of Bugs truly resembled insects pouring out of

a hive—at the rate of four thousand a day. And all were eagerly gobbled up by waiting customers around the world, including over one hundred fifty thousand by American Beetle buyers in 1959.

All of this *Wagen wunder* had been produced without what American industry considered the necessity of high-powered advertising. Until the very end of the 1950s Volkswagen's chief form of advertising was satisfied customers, word of mouth, and of course Volkswagen jokes which, after the laughs stopped, sold uncounted numbers of cars.

The feeling that Volkswagen needed advertising like Custer needed Indians was understandable, and it largely prevailed at Volkswagen of America until the advent of Dr. Carl Hahn in 1959. Like his mentor, Heinz Nordhoff, Hahn could see what army people like to call "the big picture." And the picture was that Volkswagen had the potential to move from a mere phenomenon to one of the shrinking number of dominant worldwide automotive conglomerates. For that it needed a power base, eventually new models, and even other car companies to be acquired and absorbed. And for that it needed still more sales and earnings. Thus, enter advertising.

Hahn and his associates at Volkswagen of America interviewed—or perhaps *auditioned* is a better word—dozens of representatives from the wilds of Madison Avenue. They listened to their spiels, looked at their copy and pictures, reviewed their records for other clients, and generally went home disappointed. All of the agencies more or less saw Volkswagen as basically another car account and cast their campaign ideas in the same mold of auto advertising we looked at earlier. Considering the completely different, even unique character of the Beetle, it did not take psychic abilities to see that the conventional approach would be a sharp turn into a dead-end street. The impressive reputation of American advertising had conditioned Hahn for great expectations, and he was clearly disillusioned. In interview after interview he was finding, as had some clients before him, that admen are like psychiatrists: Their time is expensive, their product is nebulous, and their help may not be immediately apparent.

What particularly perplexed and annoyed Hahn was their readiness to produce prospective or sample ads for a product they really knew little or nothing about. It was as if the formats were made up and any product could be conveniently dropped into the slot. For better or worse, the Beetle was certainly unique, and Hahn instinctively felt that some of its "uniquity" had to show through in its ads. Finally he found someone who agreed with him.

That somebody was Doyle Dane Bernbach, a ten-year-old agency, smallish by the standards of "Mad. Ave." giants, that had cut its teeth on clients like a New York department store, a popular Jewish rye bread, and a mutual fund, and later moved on to Monsanto, Polaroid, and El Al Airlines. For the latter it had produced a spectacularly successful "new departure" ad in 1957. Hired to introduce El Al's jet prop service from New York to London, the agency devised a picture of the ocean torn about four-fifths across and rolled down on the right side. In the blank space under the tear it carried the simple message: "On December 23 the Atlantic Ocean became 20% smaller." Before that airlines just didn't show pictures of open expanses of water lest passengers get the wrong impression. But instead of the wrong message, everyone seemed to get the right message from the simple, effective El Al ad, and it became famous in the business as "the torn ocean ad."

That was the kind of simplicity, straightforwardness, and basic honesty that Hahn instinctively envisioned for Volkswagen. After the preliminaries, Doyle Dane Bernbach was given a budget for 1959 of $800,000 and a virtual blank check for cooperation, understanding, and trust by Volkswagen. Their first step in the selling of the Beetle seemed a particularly intelligent one: They got to know what it was they were selling. The agency sent a contingent of copywriters, artists, and executives to Wolfsburg to see the birthing of a Beetle and to ingest the process from raw steel to the loading of Bugs onto trains and canalboats. They poked around under the 270 acres of roofed buildings, talked to as many of the nearly 44,000 workers as they could, and trudged along the hundred miles of conveyer assembly lines. When they returned to New York they knew the Volkswagen intimately, and that meant they understood that nearly everything about it was different from other cars. They learned the obvious—that it was *not* long, low, svelte, sexy, or prestigious (at least not in the conventional sense). And they learned what was not so immediately obvious to the average American driver. For

It takes this many men to inspect this many Volkswagens.

We finally came up with a beautiful picture of a Volkswagen.

A Volkswagen starts looking good when everything else starts looking bad.

Let's say it's late at night and you can't sleep. It's 10 below and you forgot to put antifreeze in your car.

(A Volkswagen doesn't use antifreeze. Its engine is cooled by air.)

Let's say it's now morning. You start your car and the gas gauge reads Empty.

(Even with a gallon left, you should go approximately 26 miles in a VW.)

Let's say you notice on your way out of the driveway that every other car on your block is stuck in the snow.

(A VW goes very well in snow because the engine is in the back. It gives the rear wheels much better traction.)

Let's say you make it into town and the only parking space is half a space between a snow plow and a big, fat wall.

(A VW will fit into half a parking space.)

Let's say it's now 9:15 a.m. and the only other guy in the office is your boss.

(Now what could be more beautiful than that?)

Dealer Name

How much longer can we hand you this line?

forever, we hope.

Because nobody ever intends to change the Volkswagen's shape.

The only reason the Volkswagen is ever changed is to make it work even better.

The money that isn't spent on outside changes is spent inside the car.

This system provides an immense advantage. Time. Years of it.

There's time to improve parts and still keep most of them interchangeable.

(Which is why it's so easy to get VW parts, and why our mechanics don't wake up screaming.)

There's time to put an immense amount of hand work into each VW, and to finish each one like a $6,000 machine.

And this system has also kept the price of the Volkswagen almost the same over the years.

Some cars keep changing and stay the same.

Volkswagens stay the same and keep changing.

Think small.

Our little car isn't so much of a novelty any more.

A couple of dozen college kids don't try to squeeze inside it.

The guy at the gas station doesn't ask where the gas goes.

Nobody even stares at our shape.

In fact, some people who drive our little flivver don't even think that about 27 miles to the gallon is going any great guns.

Or using five pints of oil instead of five quarts.

Or never needing anti-freeze.

Or racking up about 40,000 miles on a set of tires.

That's because once you get used to some of our economies, you don't even think about them any more.

Except when you squeeze into a small parking spot.

Or renew your small insurance. Or pay a small repair bill. Or trade in your old VW for a new one.

Think it over.

Dealer Name

Lemon.

This Volkswagen missed the boat.

The chrome strip on the glove compartment is blemished and must be replaced. Chances are you wouldn't have noticed it; Inspector Kurt Kroner did.

There are 3,389 men at our Wolfsburg factory with only one job: to inspect Volkswagens at each stage of production. (3000 Volkswagens are produced daily; there are more inspectors than cars.)

Every shock absorber is tested (spot checking won't do), every windshield is scanned. VWs have been rejected for surface scratches barely visible to the eye.

Final inspection is really something! VW inspectors run each car off the line onto the Funktionsprüfstand (car test stand), tote up 189 check points, gun ahead to the automatic brake stand, and say "no" to one VW out of fifty.

This preoccupation with detail means the VW lasts longer and requires less maintenance, by and large, than other cars. (It also means a used VW depreciates less than any other car.)

We pluck the lemons; you get the plums.

After 30 Volkswagens, Father Bittman still believes.

In the beginning, Father Aloysius Bittman bought a bug.

That was in 1952 when he joined the staff of St. Anthony's Indian Mission in Mandaree, North Dakota.

Since then, Father Bittman has gone a long way. In 30 Volkswagens.

Owning two or three at a time, the Bittman staff travels 600 miles per week in each. Over dirt and gravel roads and in temperatures that have been known to go to 55 below.

A couple of Volkswagens ago, Father Bittman's '65 broke through the Garrison Reservoir ice.

"It was a good time for praying," he said.

Luckily, one 255 pound priest and one

1805 pound bug floated to safety. After the ice was chopped away and a quick oil change, the good father and his faithful companion were on their way.

He was a bit peeved about the oil change though.

"It set the Mission back $1.80," complained Father Aloysius Bittman.

After a few years, it starts to look beautiful.

"Ugly, isn't it?"
"No class."
"Looks like an afterthought."
"Good for laughs."
"Stubby buggy."
"El Pig-O."

New York Magazine said: "And then there is the VW, which retains its value better than anything else. A 1956 VW is worth more today than any American sedan built the same year, with the possible exception of a Cadillac."

Around 27 miles to the gallon. Pints of oil instead of quarts. No radiator. Rear engine traction. Low insurance. $1,799* is the price. Beautiful, isn't it?

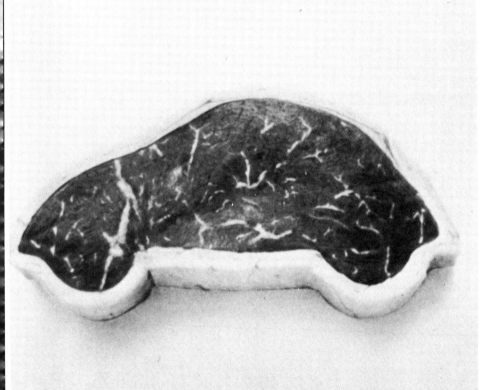

Can you still get prime quality for $1.26 a pound?

A pound of Volkswagen isn't cheap compared to other cars. But what you pay for is the quality.

Just look at what you get for your money.

13 pounds of paint, some of it in places you can't even see. (So you can leave a Volkswagen out overnight and it won't snow.)

A watertight, welded steel floor that protects against rocks,

rain, rust and rot.

Over 1,000 inspections per one Beetle.

1,014 inspectors who are so finicky that they reject parts you could easily ride around with and not even detect there was anything wrong.

Electronic Diagnosis that tells you what's right and wrong with important parts of your car.

A 1,600 cc. aluminum-magnesium engine that gets 25 miles to a gallon

at regular gasoline.

Volkswagen's traditionally high resale value.

Over 22,000 changes and improvements on a car that was well built to begin with.

What with all the care we take in building every single Volkswagen, we'd like to call it a filet mignon of a car. Only one problem. It's too tough.

Few things in life work as well as a Volkswagen.

Our car the movie star.

You are looking at the romantic lead of a big new Hollywood picture.

Please, no autographs.

The picture is Walt Disney Studio's "The Love Bug." And our VW appears (in all its real life splendor) as Herbie, the main character.

Why would a big film studio want to make a movie star out of the bug?

Why not?

Signing one up for a lifetime costs only $1,799.* That's less than they have to pay other movie stars in a single day.

Once signed up, the bug won't suddenly start making crazy demands. (A gallon of gas for every 27 miles or so is all.)

No studio could ask for a less temperamental star. (It'll work in any weather.)

Or one with fewer bad habits. (It doesn't even drink water.)

Or one that ages so gracefully.

And of course, there isn't a performer around that's better known to the public.

Who else makes three million personal appearances on the road every day?

Volkswagen ran several ads with a blank space over the caption.
In 1961 the caption read, "We don't have anything to show you in our
new model." Wolfsburg worried over the cost of buying blank space
in expensive magazines, but the idea was vindicated when people came
into dealers asking to see the little Beetle that wasn't there.
This is the 1961 Beetle that Volkswagen of America wouldn't show you.
(Volkswagen of America, Inc.)

No point in showing the '66 Volkswagen. It still looks the same.

Hardly anybody knows that the VWs in our showroom are '66s.

An eagle-eyed visitor may notice the hub caps are flattened (so they can't be scraped by curbs). But that's the only clue.

Everything else on the outside is right where we left it in '65.

Inside is another story. All our time and effort have gone into improvements that matter.

The '66 Volkswagen has a 3rd defroster in the center of the windshield for improved visibility.

We've put locks on the backs of the front seats so they can't be jolted forward.

And this year (for the first time) we've decreased the average gas mileage. By 8%. To a mere 29 miles per gallon.

Because this year (for the fourth time) we've increased the engine's power. By 25%. To give you more push per hill.

There are 23 improvements in the '66 Volkswagen.

Try and find them.

Dealer Name

5-063-1

instance, that Volkswagen had its engine in the rear, an engineering novelty unknown even in 1959 to an amazing number of people until Beetle ads made it a commonplace, or that this peculiarity offered genuine traction advantages in snow, mud, or sand. Or that it had a funny-sounding air-cooled engine which did away with such inconveniences as leaky radiators, burst hoses on lonely roads, dashing out on cold nights to add antifreeze (or cracked blocks if you forgot to), or the autumnal ritual of flushing the cooling system. Or that big fifteen-inch tires on a little car rolled forty thousand miles between replacements. Or that the standardization and stability of Volkswagen design greatly simplified spare parts and repair considerations (not to mention the fact that the disarming simplicity of the thing's insides did not tax even the most dilettante mechanic's IQ). Or that Volkswagen was possessed of the world's best parts and service organization.

They also learned what was not so immediately apparent to the casual observer. They learned of the care and personal attention that went into each car, despite the fact that Volkswagen was rapidly emerging as one of the world's great automakers, and that the ratio of inspectors to workers was the highest this side of Rolls-Royce. They even learned why this was so. The concern with quality and doing mechanical things "the correct way" had been programmed into the Teutonic psyche long before there was ever a Volkswagen or any car. That programming remained after the war, but it was mixed with a sense of defeat, despair, and shame. To say that Germans, collectively and individually, emerged from World War II with the greatest credibility problem the world has ever seen is putting it mildly. To help restore a measure of that credibility Volkswagen workers enthusiastically put their best into their work so that the product they sent out into the world would reflect on them, their new republic, and their new beginning. In their modest, mechanical way they had undertaken to prove the eighteenth-century

German philosopher Goethe wrong when he said, "I have often felt a bitter sorrow at the thought of the German people, which is so estimable in the individual and so wretched in the generality."

Doyle Dane Bernbach's trek to Wolfsburg confirmed what had already been observed about the Volkswagen, that all else aside it was viewed simply as an honest car. And, all else aside, that became the continuing theme of Volkswagen advertising: to tell it like it is—no more, no less. And that, of course, was revolutionary.

To recall the glories—and smiles—of the golden age of Beetle ads of the 1960s is better done by perusing the accompanying pages of the Beetle remembered in print than by recounting individual favorite ads. Despite their singularity the Beetle ads were not one-of-a-kind affairs; there was a common pattern, a method in the madness. As in the car itself, a natural simplicity was the dominant theme—in layout, illustrations, wording of the copy, even in the type style. While this may not have been apparent to casual observers, it became painfully obvious when others inevitably began to copy the Beetle broadsides (a good example is on page 72). First, the agency completely abandoned paintings in favor of photographs, almost always simple black and white pictures, usually without people and always with the simplest background or no background at all. There was always a headline beneath the photograph to convey the single theme of the message (e.g., "It won't drive you to the poorhouse." Or "Ugly is only skin deep." Or "After we paint the car we paint the paint."). And that line always had a plain period behind it to suggest a simple, factual statement rather than an exclamation, a pronouncement, or some message of white-paper rank.

The copy was invariably in straightforward, simple sentences—subject, verb, object—and the tone was person to person, as if the writer were talking to a friend of equal intelligence. Although perhaps a score of people contributed

What's low in upkeep, high in mileage,
maneuverable in any weather, adaptable to any terrain,
air-cooled, water-tight, trim outside, roomy inside,
equipped with three spares, precision-engineered with
42 hidden changes to date but looks the same every year?

Imitation is the most sincere form of flattery. VW's ad agency knew that it had broken virgin territory when other companies started running "Beetle ads." In the ad trade this "coattail" ad for raincoats was nicknamed "the free ride." (Volkswagen of America, Inc.)

Although we tend to forget it, there were other forms of Volkswagen advertising in addition to the clever DDB magazine ads. The Sociedade Comercial Guerin, Portugal's VW importer, made available sixty white Beetles for sixty weddings at Lisbon Cathedral on St. Anthony's Day, the favorite Portuguese wedding date. VW's version of "mass transportation" made a vivid impression on the thousands of spectators. (Volkswagen of America, Inc.)

to the ads over the years, the style remained anonymously, and indelibly, the same. In layout there were seldom symmetrical blocks of type. Sentences ended where they did and were not puffed or chopped in the "all that fits we print" style to yield an artificial neatness. Generally they went on to talk briefly about one or two features such as quality of construction, economy, rear-engine traction, easy maintenance, etc., and did not try to unload all their bombs on one target. There were few taboos, but one strict one was that the ads never directly attacked or poked fun at Detroit machines; it was considered undiplomatic, bad judgment, bad taste, and, ultimately, bad business. I can remember two ads in which an American car was pictured (actually a composite mock-up). One showed a behemoth station wagon on the left and the Volkswagen station wagon and a lone black Beetle on the right. The headline read, "For the price of some station wagons and their optional extras, you can buy a Volkswagen station wagon—and this optional extra." The other was a night shot of a garage with a big car and a Beetle in it. The copy read, "Guess which one gets to go to the party on Saturday night?"

Some Volkswagen ads were prime poster art. They drew the eye and held it long enough to deliver a message, the classic function of a poster. The eye could not help but be caught, for example, by the rear end of a Beetle penned onto a white hen's egg over the message, "Some shapes are hard to improve on." No one has yet elevated the conglomerate creators of Beetle ads into the class of Toulouse-Lautrec or Maxfield Parrish, but nevertheless people have been known to frame and hang Volkswagen ads in their homes because they were so attractive and entertaining. Odder things have made it to museum status, such as Andy Warhol's famous Campbell's soup can, and it is a safe bet that in less than fifty years whatever the nostalgic crazes are, Beetle ads will be a part of them. Beetles themselves are of course a certainty as memorabilia of an era which could produce two automobiles as different as the 1959 Volkswagen and the 1959 rocket-fin Buck Rogers Cadillac in a single twelve-month period.

It seemed inevitable that Volkswagen ads would make it to the screen. But the question was, could the proven concepts that had worked so well on the slick coated paper of *Time* and *Newsweek* and *Look* and *Life* come across with the same simple understated élan and effectiveness between Walter Cronkite and *Mission Impossible*? It was a high roller's decision, even for a company which at one point was laying out twenty-million preinflation dollars a year for advertising. However, the Beetle mystique could be translated to film, and it was. When the Beetle came to the talkies, the humility and the humor remained and people watched, waited for, talked about, told their friends about, and remembered Volkswagen commercials.

Almost everybody seemed to have a favorite he never got tired of seeing, from the one about the frugal nephew driving his Beetle in a funeral cortege of Rolls-Royces who inherits the rich uncle's estate because the old boy admired his nephew's way with a dollar to the pair of astronauts who need an exploration vehicle unaffected by heat, cold, or impossible terrain and choose 'The best car on planet Zeno.' One of the funniest was a gentle barb at all those car and gas companies who liked to show their victorious vehicles bursting through a paper barrier at the end of an economy run. The car was a Karmann Ghia, the two-seater sports version of the Beetle, and the announcer assured you that it was "the most economical sports car you can buy." When it nudges the paper barrier and fails to burst through in the usual image of TV commercial glory, he adds, "It's just not the most powerful." Perhaps the prettiest was an artistic, almost silent film of a pristine and massive snowfall seen from the windshield of a moving car. Scene after scene of spectacular crystalline winter beauty unfolds, accompanied only by the monotony of the motor. Probably ninety-five percent of the air time was totally noncommercial, unless you considered it a subliminal plug for winter sports. Then, just at the end, the Beetle is parked and its driver gets out and goes into a big snow-covered building. In a moment a snowplow emerges, and the announcer speaks his only words: "Have you ever wondered how the man who drives the snowplow drives *to* the snowplow? This one drives a Volkswagen . . . so you can stop wondering."

Of course, what may have been the very best Volkswagen commercial on film wasn't a commercial at all. It was a scene in a Woody Allen (who else?) film called *Sleeper.* The plot was that Allen dies, is frozen, and wakes up in the distant future as a sort of Rip van Winkle. Some totalitarian types are running things, and our hero of course runs afoul of them. During the inevitable chase scene he stumbles into a cave with an ancient, dusty Beetle stored in it. Naturally it starts at the turn of a key and Woody escapes the guys with the black hats, at least for the moment. The routine runs hardly longer than a real Beetle commercial (literary verisimilitude, I suppose) and is a fine example of art imitating life, or perhaps art imitating advertising—which in the case of Beetle ads may very well be the same thing.

There is a fine line between public relations and advertising. Press releases with photos like this one were sent in winter to newspaper editors, who often have space to fill or need to illustrate a winter weather story. The subtle, almost subliminal, implication is of course that VWs run well in the snow. (Volkswagen of America, Inc.)

5/The Fads

(Volkswagen of America, Inc.)

In 1972 a Detroit psychiatrist published a book intriguingly titled *Is Your Volkswagen a Sex Symbol?* In true Freudian fashion the good doctor asked a question that he never really answered, leaving the reader/patient to reach his own conclusions about that ponderous thought. In fact, for a Detroiter he didn't have too much to say about automobiles generally, and precious little about the touchstone of his title in particular—exactly one paragraph of 134 words. In those few words Dr. Jean Rosenbaum states some basic truisms about Volkswagens—that their owners are "concerned about economics, air pollution, and good craftsmanship," and that they are "individualists," and "take an intellectual and rational view of life."* More significantly, he observes that

*Used with permission of Elsevier/Nelson Books. Copyright © 1972 by Dr. Jean Rosenbaum.

The record for stuffing a single Volkswagen with humanity apparently belongs to Bournemouth College of Technology and College of Art which managed to get 103 students into and onto a Beetle and drive 15 feet. This group didn't set a record but apparently had a good time.

"When you buy a Volkswagen, you don't just get a car; you also acquire a lot of friends—other Volkswagen owners. The Volkswagen is a way of life." Disappointingly, however, the doctor fails to follow up with an analysis in depth of that important part of the Beetle mystique I have increasingly come to think of as the psychic or even mystic appeal of the Volkswagen. The master of psychic symbology, Dr. Carl Jung, would undoubtedly have recognized that the unparalleled acceptance and success of the Beetle, and especially the affection its owners often feel for it, went well beyond the simple appreciation of a good and reliable car and lapped over into what the Beetle really is—a totem.

A bit of Bavarian kitsch: A Bughouse complete with shingle roof, "timber and stucco" sides, and window boxes with flowers awaits German newlyweds. The inscribed slogans are about the same as on any other honeymoon car. (Volkswagen of America, Inc.)

Those who took college Psych I (or II) will recall that a totem is the focal point of a primeval veneration of some material object that holds a mystical place in society. The veneration creates a sort of union or fraternity among the "tribesmen" ("You don't just get a car; you also acquire a lot of friends") and is usually associated with rituals and customs (VW jokes and mileage boasts, the "art" of Beetle decoration, and the quaint ritual of cramming record numbers of college students into Beetles).

A couple of times in this book the point is made that the Volkswagen Beetle has been the most successful car in history, with twenty million of them eventually inhabiting all parts of the planet, and still counting. It is also the most noticed, receiving attention, devotion, and interest all out of proportion to its modest function as basic transportation. Other cars have performed a similar function, notably Model T and Model A Fords. To be sure, both had—and have—their devoted collectors, fanciers, replicators, and cultists. But the Beetle is another matter. Why? People seldom pay more than passing attention to utilitarian objects *in their own era*, even if years later they will pay a thousand dollars for old comic books and turn-of-the-century Coke bottles. To lapse into cliché, the Beetle was a legend in its own time, and it still is an authentic totem object. Again, why? The question would make an excellent thesis subject for a burgeoning Jungian. Does the answer lie in the unique shape? Does that odd, never-copied profile suggest something sexual, maternal, paternal—or divine? Is it the size; do Volkswagen owners feel protective because Beetles are little? But there are still smaller cars without anywhere near the curious charisma. It is because they are "ugly" and we love the ugly duckling the most? But there have been other cars, notably conceived by the French (and a few by the Americans in the early 1960s) which make the Beetle seem downright handsome. Is it the sound, that unusual purr which recalls some basic rhythm dredged up from the collective unconscious? Or do the vast numbers alone offer up the Beetle as a universal fertility symbol? The answer is that there is no answer. If we explain the mystery then we murder the mystique.

And, if there is something that the Beetle has, it is mystique—and enormous magnetism. The shape—or whatever it is—draws people and drives them to do things with Beetles, to Beetles, and for Beetles which they simply don't do with, to, and for other cars. The Volkswagen has attracted faddists better than yogurt, Frisbees, and transcendental meditation combined.

Perhaps the oddest and most persistent VW fad relates to the car's apparent affinity for water. The wartime *Schwimmwagen* was of course intended to float and navigate, but other Volkswagens just seemed to pick it up on their

Performance of the noted composition *Concerto for Yellow Volkswagen and Orchestra* by the composer Harry Phillips. This stimulating orchestral work features authentic chuffing of the Beetle engine, horn, a percussive slamming of the hood and striking of the wheel covers and bumpers. The full orchestra accompanies an English horn obbligato played from the roof of Yellow Volkswagen. (Volkswagen of America, Inc.)

Water sports, with a "waterbug," a Viking ship, and an outboard-propelled submarine conning tower.
(Volkswagen of America, Inc.)

Volkswagen's nautical racing activities are organized by The Waterbugs of America Racing Association.
The rules for amphibious competition include entering the water at speed, negotiating a mile-long water course,
and chugging back onto dry land. The thrill of victory, the gurgle of defeat. *(Small World)*

own, like a puppy's instinctive doggy paddle. The Beetle's flat bottom is sealed, the passenger compartment is fairly close to airtight (try slamming the door with the windows shut), and the air in the tires adds buoyancy. So the result is that a plain, Wolfsburg-fresh Volkswagen floated, another Beetle "uniquity." How long it would float was a question once settled by *Sports Illustrated,* which set one onto placid water in Florida and started a stopwatch. The record established was just a few seconds short of a half hour, although there are

unofficial records for considerably longer. This somewhat remarkable ability began to be noticed as more and more Volkswagens were sent off in overseas commerce and occasional Bugs were dropped into harbors around the world, surviving the dunking by bobbing around to the amusement of dock workers and the delight of newspaper photographers.

The publicity was not wasted, and a few adventuresome spirits began turning Beetles into waterbugs. In its most basic form the conversion was simple: snorkels for the air intake

That isn't just *any* Volkswagen swimming the Panama Canal; it's none other than Herbie, Walt Disney Productions' superstar of *The Love Bug* in his most recent adventure, *Herbie Goes Bananas,* wherein the four-wheeled hero thwarts smugglers and maneuvers one more romance between his human allies.

(Material from *Herbie Goes Bananas,* © 1980 Walt Disney Productions)

and exhaust, a plastic bag over the distributor, sealing the door jambs with grease, makeshift paddles for the rear wheels (or just snow tires), and a good measure of confidence—plus just a dash of insanity. A sunroof model or a convertible was also not a bad idea, just in case. A rudder wasn't needed, since turning the front wheels gave good maneuverability.

Well, what do you do with a floating Volkswagen after you've got one? Some Australians once used one to upstage a speedboat race that had been delayed because of rough water. Two Englishmen once tried to "drive" a Beetle from France to England without benefit of a ferry, only to have it swamped about ten miles across the Channel, along with their place in the Guinness book. But the most likely thing to be done by the kind of people who would go down to the sea in Volkswagens is to race them.

In America the people who organize races and lay down rules as to what is or isn't shipshape are the officials of The Waterbugs of America Racing Association. Yes, Virginia, there really is—if you don't believe it, write to them at 450 West Exchange Street, Akron, Ohio 44302, and they'll send you a soggy application form. The basic rules provide that the regatta starts on dry land, with the "ships" entering the water at full speed and then proceeding to negotiate a pylon-studded water course about a mile long. This nautical navigation fad started out with Ohio-area VW dealers, who saw a unique opportunity for some impressive advertising, and then spread to "civilians," who liked the idea of amphibious racing. The only catch is that now you have to buy a boat permit and paint your license number on the "hull," just like other yachtsmen. And then it's the thrill of victory, or the gurgle of defeat.

Strains of the Beetlemania virus, which drives victims to contest with one another in oddly metamorphosed VWs, has even been known to infect professionals who earn their daily wine, women, and song by driving fast. One such case produced what is to this day history's most ferocious Beetle.

Volkswagens have traditionally had a natural affinity for water ever since it was discovered that they float. Once two Englishmen got halfway across the Channel from France in a Beetle before abandoning "ship." But, as the sign shows, optimism springs eternal in the human—and Beetle—spirit. (Volkswagen of America, Inc.)

A favorite form of Beetle fetishism was seeing which team could push a Beetle the farthest and fastest.
(Volkswagen of America, Inc.)

The man bitten by the Bug was no less than Emerson Fittipaldi, the celebrated Brazilian Grand Prix driver. Now, in the way of introduction to this story, it could be said that Brazilians are just a little nuts about Volkswagens. There is a giant Beetle plant there which is the country's biggest single industry, and three out of four vehicles on the roads are Volkswagens. Fertile ground for the virus, which bit Fittipaldi in late 1969, having attacked his brother just a bit earlier. The effects on both were severe and took the form of a serious assault on the creation of the ultimate racing Beetle. The recipe began like all the others: "Take one serviceable Beetle," and then it went on to say, "and cut it in

half. Keep the front and throw the back half away." The back was replaced by a custom-made tubular frame holding up two 1600 cc Volkswagen engines in tandem above a Porsche transaxle. The engines were warmed up with all the hot rodder's and racer's usual legerdemain. This was a literal as well as a figurative description, since eight fired-up cylinders inside a Bug body do raise the temperature a bit. The solution was a bit bizarre, but effective (it would be crude to say crude): The windshield was tilted back to let a rush of air into the driver's compartment (i.e., the front seat), where it was scooped up and fed into four 4-inch air hoses which conveyed it to the engine. Actually, a somewhat similar

Beetle stuffing.
(Volkswagen of America, Inc.)

"Teenage Fair" offered a chance to autograph the
Beetle Beetle. (Volkswagen of America, Inc.)

The mystique of the Beetle drives owners to do things that would never enter the brains of owners of other cars. Mrs. Robert Drown of Litchfield Park, Arizona, tried to bring out the animal in a Bug by covering it with acrylic leopard skin for her daughter Melissa. Wash and wax has now become wash and comb—or blow dry. (Volkswagen of America, Inc.)

The temptation to tinker has resulted in some strictly nonissue Beetles, this one rearing up to set a record. Beetles are the most modifiable cars ever built. (Volkswagen of America, Inc.)

scoop-and-hose arrangement had been used by Dr. Porsche on the NSU people's car prototypes of the early 1930s, although of course he had the good grace not to suck air through the passenger space.

This remarkable contraption was dubbed the Fittipaldi 3200, and the whole mass of cylinders, air hoses, and oil coolers was wrapped in a fiberglass Beetle body. It was fast and fun, but what was basically a tinkerer's daydream became a racer's nightmare—*other* racers—when it got on the track. In qualifying runs at a Rio racetrack the cobbled-up Beetle outpaced a Ford GT-40 (the terror of Le Mans) and a Lola Chevrolet. Quick to reach its 120-mph four-gear speed, the fire-orange Beetle amused and astounded spectators. Since this book is more fact than fiction, we're *not* going to tell you that the Super-Super-Super-Beetle won that one-thousand-kilometer race at Guanabara back in 1969 and went on to become the progenitor of *The Beetle That Ate Indianapolis.* Not at all. But someday a Japanese filmmaker might.

American race drivers have no special immunity or resistance to the Beetle's siren call to silliness. Perhaps the ultimate Beetle racing stunt was pulled by no less than the noted vaudeville team of A. J. Foyt and Dan Gurney at Nassau Speed Week in 1964. The race itself was a minor event, a one-hundred-mile run for standard issue Volkswagens; but Gurney had sneaked in a much-modified machine capable of chewing up every other car in the race. However, instead of heading for the lead early on in the race, he pulled up on A. J.'s bumper and *pushed* him. In fact, he pushed him past every other car in the race and kept him there for much of the hundred miles. Then, just before the finish, Gurney passed his partner and finished first, fully expecting the disqualification which would surely come, and he watched with a smile while the quizzical judges awarded first place to number two, who really hadn't tried hard at all.

As the Beetle proliferated (at the rate of one every

fifteen seconds by 1964) and every member of the "tribe" could have his very own totem if he wanted it, some odd wrinkles in the original liturgy of austerity, quality, and sobriety appeared. Some of them involved quaint folk curiosities like seeing how fast various teams of "worshippers" could push a Beetle around a track, or how many college students could be crammed into a Volkswagen; a very popular new form of devotion indeed, especially if the stuffees were coed. The record appears to have been set in England by students of the Bournemouth College of Technology and College of Art, who got 103 students into and onto a Beetle "and held their breath while the car was driven fifteen feet." The old record had been set in Graz, Austria, with a mere 57 passengers carried the same distance. Even something like a mystery cult appeared, with adherents who paid their devotion by stuffing Beetles with crumpled newspaper. It took ten of them thirty minutes to stuff a car with fifty pounds of paper, and then forty-five minutes to unstuff it. There's a deep symbology there . . . maybe.

The fertility cult got a boost from new converts around the world. Typical were reports like one from the Sydney *Sun Herald* in Australia, which read: "Recently, a businessman parking at Mascot Airport noticed a couple cuddling in the next car, a Volkswagen. He flew to Melbourne, returned to Sydney the same day, and found the same couple in the same Volkswagen still cuddling." At the other end of the globe in Liège, Belgium, a young thing named Olga Springel backed her car into the front of Charles Brucke's Beetle. She offered her insurance company's name and, at the very least, a cup of coffee while the potential plaintiff scribbled notes. Then there was lunch, a call on the insurance agent, then—so the day shouldn't be a total loss—dinner and dancing. And, on the stroke of midnight, a marriage proposal and acceptance. The mystique of sex and the single Volkswagen isn't confined to human species. A few years ago a Beetle accidentally got shoved into Nevada's Lake Mead and,

The Abominable Snow Beetle was created by the South African Department of Transportation for an expedition to the South Pole. Heavy-duty skis on the front worked well for steering, and wide cleated tires on the rear provided plenty of traction. Sort of the ultimate snowmobile. (Volkswagen of America, Inc.)

Two can live as cheaply as one, provided they both drive Beetles.

(Volkswagen of America, Inc.)

A Wisconsin VW dealer named Carl Schneider got this idea while toying with two plastic Volkswagen models. Eighteen months later the world's only Volkswagen dual-cowl phaeton in the grand classic tradition of the 1930s was born. (So why shouldn't a double Beetle have a double gestation period?) It is real, and eminently practical for the owner with champagne tastes and a beer budget. Delta Imports rents it out for special occasions, and it has made the pages of everything from the *National Enquirer* to the London *Times.* (Courtesy Carl Schneider, Delta Import Motors, Inc., La Crosse, Wisconsin)

according to the *Las Vegas Review Journal*, "was followed ashore by several romantic turtles when it was pulled out."

After more than coincidental numbers of babies seemed to be getting born in the backseats of Volkswagens, the company decided to go along with the fertility-symbol image by offering what may be the motor industry's oddest rebate: the "Bonds for Babies Born in Beetles" offer. A bona fide Beetle Baby gets a one-hundred-dollar bond, and about twenty a year collected. (The program is now called "Born in Bunnies.") One New Orleans newborn missed out, however, when his father called a dealer to check on the offer.

Sleepy-eyed, the guy said yes, and he thought it was $25. "Oh," said the voice on the other end. "Is that all? Excuse me while I get my old lady out of the car." That is, if he could. An Oakland, California, newspaper columnist writing about Beetle Babies observed that "Once a very pregnant woman gets into the back of a VW, giving birth may be the only way to get out."

As the Beetle became a household commonplace familiar from Hudson's Bay to Antarctica, it evolved into a standard of measure rather like the king's foot or the universal distance from nose to fingertip. Around the world people found themselves speaking not in abstracts of liters, kilos, pounds, miles, or kilometers, but in phrases like "the size of a Volkswagen," or "enough power to run a hundred VWs for five years," or "a Volkswagen-sized flying mammal." Military and NASA public relations writers seemed especially fond of measuring things in Volkswagens. Floods of phrases like these flowed from federal typewriters during the golden Beetle years:

The first stage of the Titan engine generates 430,000 pounds of thrust, the equivalent of the thrust of 219,000 Volkswagens.

The 16-inch guns of the U.S.S. *New Jersey* can, in effect, hurl a Volkswagen with enough force to penetrate 30 feet of reinforced concrete. [But not even a guess at the body and fender estimate.]

You could drive a VW 2-1/2 times around the world on the fuel needed for a Boeing 707 for one hour.

A nuclear engine will be developed that will generate 5,000 megawatts—the power output of 50,000 Volkswagens, a noted space scientist says.

A Volkswagen could travel to the moon 8,656 times one way or 24 times every day on the amount of aircraft fuel pumped out of McGuire Air Force Base during 1966.

And then there was the fellow who had never heard about too much of a good thing, who wrote that:

Lockheed's giant C-5 jet transport is so big that it can hold 100 Volkswagens and carries enough fuel to drive a VW for more than a hundred years. . . . The engine nacelles are so big— both in length and diameter—that each could garage a couple of Beetles.

In 1974, when saving gas began to take on new meaning, Beetles were of course the natural standard of measure.

Someone at Volkswagen of America was turned loose with an eleven-digit calculator and some estimates that there were approximately one hundred million cars in the U.S. which traveled an average of ten thousand miles per year each. This gave him a total of one trillion miles, divided by the average gas consumption of 22.9 miles per gallon per Beetle versus 13.6 miles per gallon for the average American car, and he came up with the news that if everyone drove a Beetle the U.S. would save 29,861,289,494 gallons of gas a year.

The comparisons continued even after the Beetle disappeared from the showrooms. A candidate for an all-time favorite Beetle measure has to be a report in the San Diego *Evening Tribune* that the Agua Caliente Race Track was giving away two hundred thousand free margaritas made from a million ounces of tequila, which concluded with the line: "A VW Beetle gassed to the same degree would travel about 195,000 miles."

Once there was a French aristocrat who so loved his Bugatti sports car that he couldn't bear to part with it even when he bought a newer and faster one. He reasoned that this creation of the master Ettore Bugatti was not only a work of art to be preserved, but also that to discard it after years of faithful service would be a barbaric act of ingratitude. So he knocked a hole in the wall of his chateau, rolled the little machine in onto a Persian carpet, and then had the wall rebuilt. Now, so far as we know, nobody has waxed quite *that* devoted to a Beetle. But it is not the first time that a car has made its contribution to the fine arts. *
There is, for example, the noted composition *Concerto for Yellow Volkswagen and Orchestra* by the composer Harry Phillips. This stimulating orchestral work features authentic

---

*Other devotees have converted Beetles into coffee tables, wall decorations, kid's play houses, and even tool sheds!

Herbie "breaks into the big time" in *The Love Bug,* wherein he adopts a down-on-his-luck race driver who reluctantly but eventually comes to realize that Herbie is not exactly your everyday Beetle. With a mystical mind of his own, Herbie vanquishes villains right and left and even finds the right lady love for his "owner."

That lovable Love Bug Herbie is back—and he's as heroic as ever. Here he high jumps to escape from ruthless security guards during an exciting San Francisco chase sequence from *Herbie Rides Again*, Walt Disney's comic sequel to *The Love Bug*. (Material from *Herbie Rides Again*, © 1974 Walt Disney Productions)

"It's a bird! It's Jaws! No, it's Herbie!" A dream sequence from *Herbie Rides Again*, in which adventure Herbie saves historic San Francisco from the ravages of real estate developers, and of course fosters another romance. (Material from *Herbie Rides Again*, © 1974 Walt Disney Productions)

chuffing of the Beetle engine, horn, a percussive slamming of the hood, and striking of wheel covers and bumpers. The full orchestra accompanies an English horn obbligato played from the roof of the yellow Volkswagen.

The Bugatti-loving Frenchman had nothing on a loyal American lady who stood by her veteran Volkswagen through thick and thin—and through restoration, accident, epic battles with insurance moguls, and rerestoration. Eileen Waldron of East Haven, Connecticut, is one of those people who believe that, like a diamond, a Volkswagen is forever. She purchased a new Bug in 1965 and lived with it for 221,000 miles, replacing only clutch and muffler. A replacement engine and general sprucing up carried the little car past the quarter-million-mile mark before disaster struck in the form of a truck which hit from the rear with devastating force, breaking the transmission, cracking the crankshaft,

and inflicting other assorted trauma. Ms. Waldron promptly had her Beetle wheeled into general automotive surgery, and two thousand dollars later he was his hale and hearty self. Then the battle for the bill began with the liable driver's insurance company. Ignoring the basic principle of insurance law that "the injured party shall be after the event as before," the adjustor sneered that a Volkswagen has a life expectancy of seven years and this one had been running on borrowed time for five years. It was so old, he reasoned, that it wasn't even listed in that bible of automotive valuation, the National Automobile Dealers' Association manual. Therefore, he lectured, insurance companies automatically consider such pariahs worth one hundred dollars (including, presumably, 1930 Duesenberg dual-cowl phaetons commanding a quarter of a million dollars at auction, or Queen Elizabeth's Rolls-Royce). The gauntlet had been flung in the face

Herbie, *The Love Bug*, became a Disney "cartoon" character who regularly vanquished villains and smoothed the road to romance in approved G-rated Hollywood fashion. Here Herbie carries newlyweds Ken Berry and Stephanie Powers past an honor guard of rearing Beetles. Only in Hollywood—and only with a Beetle. (Material from *Herbie Rides Again*, © 1974 Walt Disney Productions)

Dare we call him "the two-door matador"? Herbie takes on a lot of bull in the arena and, of course,
Old Number 53 comes through again.

(Material from *Herbie Goes Bananas*, © 1980 Walt Disney Productions)

of Ms. Waldron's Yankee sense of thrift and justice, and the battle lines were drawn up. She sued.

An astute judge overruled the motion of the insurance company's lawyer for a dismissal of the two-thousand-dollar damage claim as "excessive," recognizing that the NADA Blue Book value of a car is merely a general guide and had little or no meaning past the first several years of a car's useful life—which for a Beetle may be when the last Timex stops ticking. As the case moved on—and on—the company set up surveillance on Ms. Waldron and assembled a dossier to discourage her defense of her beloved Beetle. Undaunted, she escalated the battle into the media; and a newspaper and radio and TV stations ran a series of articles and reports considering the other side of insurance fraud—*by* insurers. Local accounts of legal skirmishes and broadsides continued and eventually made a national wire service under the headline "VW Owner Tells Insurance Company to Bug Off." A move to warm legal hearts from Bryan to Bailey was the plaintiff's discovery of the same insurance company's supervisor offering his *own* nearly nine-year-old non-Blue Book-listed Beetle for sale at twenty-five hundred dollars. A bit of a crack in "the rock," a leak in "the umbrella," or mothhole in "the blanket."

When the jury came back, Eileen Waldron had won her case against the insurance company. She had sued for a total of $17,000, including medical, and settled for $16,500.

Both Papa Volkswagen in Wolfsburg and its American offspring in Englewood Cliffs, New Jersey, have been just a bit circumspect about the multifarious fads to which their product has fallen heir, even though Heinz Nordhoff himself may have invented the first of the Volkswagen fads in the early 1950s by awarding a gold watch and a congratulatory letter to owners who got past one hundred thousand kilometers. The company has gone along with some things, like the Babies Born in Beetles gimmick and the Gold Bug Special Edition, but by and large it has sat back and smiled

Eileen Waldron's 1965 VW may be the most heroic Beetle since *Herbie*, taking on single-handedly the corporate colossus of the insurance industry. The car was hit in the rear by a truck and restored, but the truck's insurer refused to pay the repair bills, claiming that a VW's life expectancy is seven years and that Ms. Waldron's Beetle was running on borrowed miles. Lengthy litigation ensued, with the case getting extensive national media coverage.
(Courtesy Eileen Waldron)

while people bought Beetles and did strange things with, to, and in them. Their greatest concession has been to chronicle some of the madness in *Small World*, Volkswagen of America's magazine for Beetle owners. Never has it occurred to Volkswagen to *start* a fad, and when it even looked like things might get trendy with a general purpose VW utility vehicle in the early 1970s, the company waged a small battle to keep it out of the U.S. market. Naturally, VW aficionados being what they are, the company lost.

The vehicle, officially the Type 181, was an updated version of the old wartime *Kübelwagen*, a four-door convertible, ascetic, two-cents-plain machine that lets you get to know

License plates which double as small billboards say it all about the way Beetle owners feel. (*Small World*—both pages)

what basic transportation *really* means. (Volkswagen of America dubbed it "The Thing.") NATO forces used some, there were sales to rugged, underdeveloped parts of the planet, and even the Chinese army showed some interest.

The Type 181 was part of Volkswagen's diversification program of the late 1960s, and the fairly low-volume operation was moved to the Mexican plant in August 1972 where it is still being made. Although a strictly business machine, the 181 was, well, kind of cute. Its boxy front end now concealed the spare tire which had been carried right out on the old sloped *Kübelwagen* hood, and it had neat angular fenders, more power, and all the other improvements inherited from the Beetle. And it also had the old virtues of ignoring heat and cold, mechanical accessibility and simplicity, fine traction, *and* an eight-inch road clearance. It was, in effect, a natural off-the-road machine for rugged terrain, what certain masochists like to call a recreational vehicle. American motoring journalists called for the *Kübelwagen* (Volkswagen strenuously avoided calling it that) in the American market, but Volkswagen shook its head in the belief that the bare Beetle itself was already too austere for the American market. In July 1971, *Motor Trend* ran an article which said, in headline, "We liked the 181 as soon as we saw it but VWA doesn't think we need it," and suggested "a few letters." Volkswagen polled its dealers, who voted no, but the cry would not be stilled and by early 1973 dealers were stocking the 181— merrily promoted as The Thing—and one more Beetle fad was born.

Rarely has there breathed a Beetle owner who has not, at some time or other, felt that his car had some sort of personality of its own. Beetles sometimes tend to give the impression that they are some sort of a four-wheeled leprechaun or, more appropriately, the spirit of some Black Forest elf settled into steel and springs. Even those not easily given to such romantic notions have sensed a subtle persona about their little car as it makes its appointed rounds. Well, that

being the case, it was inevitable that those masters of attributing human characteristics to nonhuman entities—Walt Disney Productions—would eventually pick up on the Volkswagen. The result was a sort of motorized Mickey Mouse; Herbie as *The Love Bug*, a film that surprised everybody but Herbie by becoming the highest grossing picture of 1969, and which grew into three more delightful movies. In those follow-ups the supporting players change but Herbie (and his twenty-six stand-ins) always plays Herbie, the elfin hero who vanquishes villains and smooths the road to romance. In both fiction and fact Herbie confirms what we were saying earlier about the irresistible, psychic attraction of Beetles. *The Love Bug*'s producer, Bill Walsh, had not settled on a "star car" for the role, so he parked several candidates outside the Disney studio commissary and watched people's reactions. He recalls, "As the employees passed on their way to lunch they looked at the little cars, kicked the tires, and turned the steering wheels. But everybody who went by *patted* the Volkswagen. They didn't pat the other cars, which was indicative. The Volkswagen had a personality of its own that reached out and embraced people. Thus we found our star." From there it was the classic unknown-to-superstar-overnight success story.

From *The Love Bug* to *Herbie Rides Again* to *Herbie Goes to Monte Carlo* and on to the newest *Herbie Goes Bananas,* the stories carry the basic theme of Herbie as a sort of lovable, mechanical Don Quixote righting wrongs and moonlighting as a matchmaker. Money is, of course, the furthest thing from his motorized mind, but Walt Disney accountants can account for $200 million in box office receipts from Herbie's films, and see "the series as one of the most successful in the history of motion pictures." Like other superstars, he even has his foot—er, tire—prints in the concrete outside Grauman's Chinese Theatre in Hollywood. Perhaps only the Disney organization could make a folk hero out of a small car, but then only a Beetle could have played the part.

6/The Canvas Volkswagen

To some people a virgin Volkswagen is what a piano was to Chopin, ceilings to Michelangelo, or a pretty senorita to Don Juan. That is, they find it difficult to keep their hands off. For them a Wolfsburg-fresh VW is a clean canvas, a starting point for self-expression, a medium, a challenge.

That challenge has been met in thousands of creative, cute, curious, crazy, corny, colorful, and downright cockamamy ways. No one seems to have recorded the first strokes of the artist's hand on a Beetle, but then who knows who made

Double vision. In the Grotemarkt of Groningen, Holland, an artist has welded together two Beetle bodies, floor pan to floor pan, with one set of wheels in between, and set it on four steel legs to create an eye-filling, mind-jogging piece of Volks-art.
(Volkswagen of America, Inc.)

Half-scale sand Beetle built for The Great Sand Castle Contest of Carmel. (Volkswagen of America, Inc.)

the first scrawlings on a cave wall? The significant thing
is that both were inevitable. One way man expresses himself is
by decorating his environment, and there can be little argument
that the Bug became a very real part of that environment.
The itch to say something with a Volkswagen has sometimes
been scratched in fairly simple, straightforward ways,
such as the flower children of Haight-Ashbury (and their
successors in title) who painted daisies on their doors,
five-branched serrated marijuana leaves on the fenders, and
inverted distress-signal American flags on the hoods. The

psychedelic motifs were simply another form of "the medium is
the message" litany. About the same time, European kids
were usually a little more restrained in their expression (or
perhaps more respectful of the price of paint jobs). Most opted
for either crossed-eyes decals appearing at the bottom of
VW hood lids or the ubiquitous "ugly duckling" decals, which
could be spotted in student havens from Schwabbing
to the Dam square to the beaches of Bari.

However, decals and daisies were only for dilettantes.
The soul of the artist cried out for much more than an

One way to freeze gas prices. The snow-bug was sculpted by a team of art teachers for the Cooperstown, New York, Winter Festival.
(Volkswagen of America, Inc.)

afternoon of soak-straighten-stroke with decals or daubing in some leftover enamel pots. The more thoughtful planned their projects with graph paper and scale models, like a Mr. Parnell of Cody, Wyoming, who planned to present his wife with a new orange Bug with a ladybug's black spots. When the motif looked OK on paper, Parnell went on to painting a Tonka-toy Beetle to get a three-dimensional perspective. Finally he progressed to the real thing, with delicately feminine eyelashes over the headlights, and the inscription "The Lady's Bug."

Beetle artists have hardly stopped at the medium of mere paint to make their statements. A half-scale sand sculpture of the familiar profile has been entered in The Great Sand Castle Contest of Carmel (California). And in a colder climate a full-scale Snow Bug was sculptured by a team of art teachers for the Cooperstown, New York, Winter Festival. There has even been a Rubber Bug, the contemporary soft sculpture of graduate art student Sid Rennels. The "skin" was created by painting a real Beetle with layers of latex, peeling it off, stuffing the skin with shredded foam rubber, and painting the detail of windows, headlights, and hardware. If not sculpture, it was at least the world's largest throw pillow (page 106).

In other works of art the VW itself, or parts of it, have become legitimate sculpture. In the Grotemarkt of Groningen, Holland, an artist has welded together two Beetle bodies, floor pan to floor pan, with one set of wheels in between, and set it on four steel legs to create an eye-filling, mind-jogging piece of Volks-art (page 99). Perhaps one of the most creative uses of Volkswagen parts in sculpture is "The Volks-Maiden of Savsjostrom." Its Swedish creator, Allan Alsterhed, started with the floor pan of a well-traveled 1950 Beetle and then just rearranged things into suitably feminine shapes. When does a Beetle become a spider? When Reno, Nevada, artist Dave Fambrough exchanges wheels for welded sections of irrigation pipe to give the Beetle body six spider legs.

Anything that captures the attention and fancy of the American public is not likely to escape the concerned interest of those compulsive takers of the popular pulse, the advertising agencies. If people were irresistibly drawn to decorate VWs to play out all the prides and passions of their souls, "Why," reasoned a classic adman's mind at the Reuben H. Donnelley agency, "couldn't that primeval urge be turned to promoting a product?" A client was found in Canada Dry's Wink, a new citrus-based soft drink, and in 1969 the Donnelley people gleefully distributed "Paint Your Wagon" (!) entry blanks, inviting contestants to design their dream Beetle right up from the innermost recesses of their psyches. The venture proved to be sort of the ad industry's equivalent of playing with DNA molecules, nuclear power plants, or Iranian politicians—that is, nobody knew what to expect next. Donnelley expected a routine response from "a run-of-the-mill coloring contest with not too large a volume of returns since it was a specialized skill contest with an appeal mainly for people interested in art," or so the account

"The Volks-Maiden of Savsjostrom" (Sweden) is said to be made from a worn-out 1950 Beetle, but the rumor is that she's really R2-D2's mother. (Volkswagen of America, Inc.)

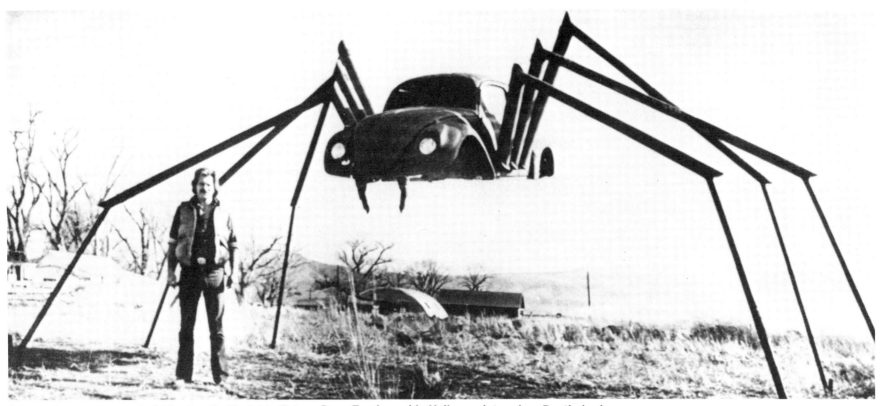

Suggesting a scene out of *The Beetle That Ate Tokyo*, Dave Fambrough's Volks-sculpture is a Beetle body welded to lengths of irrigation pipe. He plans his next work as a centipede made from a boxcar. *Ars gratia artis* is what MGM says. (World Wide Photos, Inc.)

exec thought. The contestants themselves expected a total of fifty-five new Beetles, and they were the only ones who got what they expected.

Donnelley found itself deluged with 35,364 entries, and the panel of art teachers hired to hack its way through them discovered that it had stepped into a great endless swamp of Volks-fantasy. Some entries were commercial—Wink bottle caps for wheels on Beetles covered by winking eyes— but most were not. Some were regional-oriented art. A Hawaiian entrant covered the car in lush rain-forest foliage with a giant snail curled around the rear fender wells. On the other

side of the country a Pennsylvania entrant turned the simple line drawing on the entry blank into a piece of Amish folkart with distelfinks, hex signs, and Pennsylvania Dutch geometrics. Another came decked out like a Beetle-shaped Persian carpet.

But the challenge to the indigenous Volks-artist could hardly be fully extended on a small paper entry blank. Donnelley had created a Frankenstein, and their account executive contacted his client, perhaps a little glassy-eyed, to say that the agency was receiving "many unusual entries involving lights, motors, many media such as clay, metal wires, etc. plus three 'mural' entries" in which the contestants took "decorate the

The Lady Bug paint job for Fern Parnell of Cody, Wyoming, started out on a Tonka-toy baby Bug and then grew to the real thing. (*Small World*)

There is something magnetically appealing about the Beetle that attracts artists from high school art classes to serious sculptors, and the Beetle is very likely the subject of more artistic endeavors than any other automobile. Here, an art class from Eastern Christian High School in Paterson, New Jersey, puts the finishing touches on a papier-mâché Bug. (Volkswagen of America, Inc.)

Cross-eyed Beetles were ubiquitous around student havens throughout Europe. (Author's photo)

The Rubber Bug, a contemporary soft sculpture by Sid Rennels of Southern Illinois University. The "skin" was created by painting a real Beetle with layers of latex, peeling it off, stuffing the skin with shredded foam rubber, and painting in the detail of windows, headlights, and hardware. (Southern Illinois University—Carbondale—News Service)

Volkswagen" literally and created a design the actual size of a Volkswagen. One man delivered his entry by hand all the way from Massachusetts so that it would not be damaged in transit. It consisted of a "framed picture painted on velvet depicting a Volkswagen traveling across a desert complete with cacti and flashing colored lights." Another imaginative contestant created a VW of delicate design made from black wires mounted on a large block of polished wood. One entrant built a screened box through which a Volkswagen could be seen against moving scenery. There was even one design made completely of dried pieces of the ingredients used in the manufacture of Wink—slices of lemon for wheels, grapefruit rind, etc. Finally, there was a large framed entry that used a Wink bottle as a spaceship ejecting a Volkswagen.

The outpouring of interest in Beetles as graphic art objects won new Beetles for fifty-five Volks-artists to ply their talents on. But to the serious observer in the advertising world the episode was vastly more valuable. It served to firmly establish the principle that there was something psychically magnetic about the Beetle that drew people's attention, and that decorated Beetles drew that attention even more magnetically.

This discovery was not lost on one Charlie E. Bird of Los Angeles, a marketing consultant who had taken unto himself the task of taking billboards off the roadsides and putting them on the road—on the sides of cars. The idea was hardly new; there were ads of the sides of horse-drawn omnibuses a century and a half ago, and today it is hard to find a mass-transit bus anywhere on which its governmental owners have not tried to cash in on the value of mobile ads. In the early 1970s Bird had been experimenting with ads painted or decaled onto various kinds of private cars. After a while the obvious became clear to him: People paid more attention to painted Beetles than to any other car. Inspiration struck and Bird envisioned gaily colored fleets of

mixed medium-message Beetles circumnavigating the freeways and byways of the world. There was a modest start of a hundred Beetles, hardly more than a "chuffle" in Beetlese,* carrying catchy graphic art ads decaled over electric bright paint jobs. The combination virtually guaranteed double takes on the road and in parking lots, and such is the warp and woof of the advertising business—first, you have to get their attention. The clients for those hundred vivid Volkswagens—United Airlines, *Time* magazine, and Sony— were no small-timers seeking a one-shot-in-the-arm pitch for Saturday's big special at Al's Pizzeria. They were not disappointed with their visibility factor, and Bird has never looked back from those first hundred Bugs in 1972. Neither, except for Volkswagen buses, has he looked at any other medium for carrying the message—and willing owners have offered him every other kind of car you can think of, up to and including Rolls-Royces.

This particular corner of the medium needed a name, and what better for Beetles carrying built-in billboards than "Beetleboards"? The name caught on almost as fast as the idea. As Beetleboards grew from the hundreds to the thousands (well over ten thousand total in the U.S. so far) the idea of "cute" soft-sell rolling ads acquired the reputation of one of the most inoffensive advertising techniques ever devised, especially in an industry not exactly revered for inoffensiveness or even taste. ABC-TV watched Beetleboards drive by and found them as unobjectionable as an old house dog: "There is nothing bad we can say about Beetleboards. They are colorful, attention-getting, decorative, effective, they're housebroken, and they don't eat much." Their rivals over at CBS waxed

---

*Wolves come in packs, fish in schools, fighter planes in squadrons, cows in herds, locusts in plagues, etc. So what should you call a batch of Beetles? That question posed a quandary until somebody reflected on the unique sound of a Beetle's air-cooled engine taking off in first gear, a distinctive sort of "chuffing" sound. Thus among Bug fanciers was coined the collective form, "a chuffle of Volkswagens."

Vanguard Beetleboard

Ultra-Brite Beetleboard

Zack Beetleboard

CBS-TV once called Beetleboards "nothing less than the greatest advertising idea in history."
The thing began in 1972 with a Los Angeles adman named Charles Bird; the
popularity of cute little cars covered with zippy graphics (for clients' cash, of course)
has paralleled the success of the Beetle itself. (Beetleboards International)

serious and pronounced Beetleboards "nothing less than the greatest advertising idea in history." Not a bad compliment from an outfit whose stock-in-trade is TV commercials.

Charlie Bird does not get his Beetles through a private pipeline into Wolfsburg; they are privately owned and fed and housed by their own Volks-folks. Which brings up the question, Why in the world would anyone let some L. A. adman paint his Bug a screeching loud color and stick ads all over it? Beetleboard drivers do get paid with a new paint job, twenty-five dollars a month for "circulating and scintillating" (not hard if you're electric lime or bilious blue), twenty-five dollars a day for participation in special events (and sometimes samples of the sponsor's wares)—up to one thousand dollars total in cash and merchandise over a two-year contract. The attention lovers among them also get a dividend of more stares and smiles than the drivers of new Rolls-Royces.

And then there is what might be called The Aphrodisiac Factor. No one has often accused the lowly Beetle of having much sex appeal, but apparently something sensual happens when you put ads on them. Once Beetleboards got into circulation, Bird started getting letters like these:

Hi Beetleboard People,

Ever since my old beige Bug was transformed into a snappy yellow pair of "Just Jeans" my life has changed. The guys on my campus used to ignore me but [not any more]. Naturally, they all want to go out in my car, but I don't care as long as I get to go out. Even my dog gets more dates since he's been seen in my Beetleboard.

Hello Beetleboards,

A funny thing happened last week. An identical [Beetleboard] to mine was parked downtown. My roommate spotted it and climbed in to wait for a ride home. Imagine the confusion when the car's real owner came along! Once they straightened things out they had a good laugh and since they've been dating regularly.

Dear Beetleboards,

Would you believe my girl and I got married in our White Stag Beetleboard? I met her last winter in Aspen. We're both skiers but it was my car that attracted her attention. She loved the crazy graphics. Anyway, we went steady all spring and summer and when we decided to tie the knot we felt it was only fitting that it should be in the vehicle that brought us together.

Tramps Beetleboard

Jack-In-The-Box Beetleboard

Olympia Beer Beetleboard

Charles E. Bird, president of Beetleboards of America, Inc. (Beetleboards International)

It was not entirely a unique occurrence, for the "promotion in motion" qualities of Beetleboards seem to work for more than just the paying clients. In Boulder, Colorado, a couple met while their Beetles were going through the paint shop and they were married three months later (the couple, not the Beetles). Even a Beetleboard dressed staidly in *Time* magazine covers evoked inquiries if there were Beetleboards advertising *Playboy* or *Penthouse*. There aren't so far, but if Bird ever signs them up the temptation to label them, "Gentlemen, start your engines!" would be hard to resist.

From the beginning, finding people to sacrifice their Beetles on the altar of mammon and Madison Avenue was not difficult, which seems to say more for the inherently unique character of Beetles and Beetle owners than it does for twenty-five dollars a month. Today, there are about eight thousand Beetleboards rolling the roads of America (and seventy-five thousand applications from people who want them), plus about two thousand pristine white "Beetleboard Bulletins"

which can shed their decals as often as every two months. And now the sun never sets on Beetleboards; they chuff the roads of North and South America, Europe, and even Asia, extolling the merits of both their sponsors and themselves.

Back in 1978 *The New York Times* wondered what "Beetleboards of America, Inc., get[s] out of all this pop art effort?" They did some quick calculating based on 1978 figures of 5,200 cars costing advertisers an average of $140 a month for six months and came up with gross figures of close to nine million dollars a year. That's a lot of money for being cute, but then Mickey Mouse didn't do so badly either. There were a lot of early years when Heinz Nordhoff would have been very happy with that figure for the whole Volkswagen operation. What must the ghost of old Dr. Porsche think of what has come of his homely little "people's car," from creative inspiration to grand scheme gone awry to industrial phenomenon to cultural artifact to art object to Beetleboard?

(Beetleboards International)

GWG Beetleboard

7/A Rose by Another Name

The Cimbria SS has a shape that would turn heads on the Via Veneto, but the Italian-influenced super sports body sits atop an ordinary Beetle chassis. (Amore Cars, Ltd.)

There was once a time when a man bought a new car in much the same way that he bought a new suit from a bespoke tailor. He called at a clublike showroom where he was treated as a client rather than merely a customer, and where the several cars on display were simply the hors d'oeuvres before the main meal, to be selected from an endless menu of delectables. The client considered the "mechanicals" on the showroom sample, if that's what turned him on; if the chassis was fast enough, quiet enough, or smooth enough he would consider what kind of body would be built for his car. The starting point was to leaf through the master catalog and peruse the roadsters, the convertible victorias, the all-weather sedans, the phaetons, the convertible berlines, the town sedans, or the all-weather town landaus. For example,

the Duesenberg catalog of the early 1930s displayed eighteen models by seven different coach builders. But the client was hardly limited by that minuscule sampling. Perish the thought. He had his own choice of any other custom coach builder, domestic or foreign; his freedom of materials, colors, and whatever foibles or fancies he wanted to indulge: a special compartment for the family Afghan hound, an in-built toilet, an electric stove, or the more usual marquetry liquor cabinet or Elizabeth Arden vanity case for milady. No detail was too small for attention. Terence Rattigan's film *The*

A Beetle body drops onto its chassis at Wolfsburg. The Beetle is the last car to keep the separate body-chassis construction after other builders have gone over to unitized construction. There would be no kit-car industry without it. (Volkswagen of America, Inc.)

Yellow Rolls-Royce opens with Rex Harrison as the Marquess of Frinton contemplating a new Phantom. There are, however, a few irritants. Fingering the crystal in the backseat bar, he murmurs to the coach builder's salesman, "I don't much care for the shape of that decanter. And the telephone is badly placed. I want it on the left side. Also, that seat is about one inch too long."* The client, or course, got what he wanted, and the big yellow and black Rolls glides off to cinematic glory to the tune of Riz Ortolani's grandiose theme music.

      In the heyday of the genuine custom car it was often a case of everyman his own designer, and his car became

an accurate expression of a piece of his true personality. What made this possible was the fact that cars were built initially as a chassis, a ladderlike steel frame with four wheels and an engine and steering wheel which—with a crude seat attached—could actually be driven. From the side rails of the frame a series of body hangers projected out, and onto these were laid the body, built separate and apart from the chassis, perhaps even in another city or country. For instance, a Duesenberg chassis built in Indianapolis often carried a body built by Murphy coach builders in Pasadena, California. Perhaps not the most efficient system, but it created cars that have survived as legitimate works of art representing the artistic high watermark of the motorcar. Perhaps the greatest virtue of the coach-building system was that it allowed the chassis builder to concentrate on what he knew best—

---

* From *The Yellow Rolls-Royce* by Jack Pearl, copyright 1965. Used with permission, Simon & Schuster, New York

the mechanicals of engine, brakes, suspension, etc.—and left the consideration of line, leather, and lacquer to a specialist of another sort.

Now, you ask, what has all this to do with a modest little machine whose very name—"people's car"—suggests the essence of egalitarianism, and which was ground out with the unvarying uniformity of German link sausages? Well, a great deal more than may first appear. The coach-building system began to be absorbed into the big automobile corporations (with names surviving to this day in model designations like Fleetwood and Le Baron) even before cars lost their separate frames to unit construction in which the body, in essence, *becomes* the frame. Once the frame disappeared as a separate entity there could be no more true custom cars as an industry, only modifications of factory-built ones. Now, there are arguments pro and con about this development, but the most significant one is that the method is the most efficient—read cheap—way to build a car, and therefore now universal.

For all his brilliant efforts at cutting the cost of the people's car, Dr. Porsche did not invent unitized construction; that was a British development some years later. The chassis system was the only known way to build a car in the early 1930s, but it was too heavy for the Volkswagen concept. So what Porsche did was to make the frame of the Volkswagen a flat steel pan, corrugated for strength but light in weight. It is what gives the Beetle such a nice, neat, smooth bottom and what makes it nearly watertight. The Beetle body is bolted onto this pan frame with eighteen bolts on each side. It is also what made possible the radically different looking Karmann Ghia (although the chassis is not identical) and, in fact, the early Porsche sports cars. The factories at Wolfsburg and elsewhere were created to replicate the pan-frame design and continued to produce it in astronomical numbers long after other makers had gone over to unitized construction. Because of the unique design of the Volkswagen it was

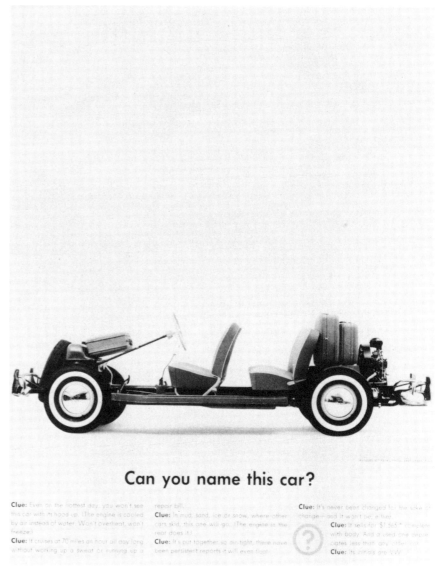

Can you name this car?

The Volkswagen's unique pan-chassis construction allowed the body to be completely detached by unbolting it from the frame, and permitted another completely different body to be bolted on in its place. This feature single-handedly created the kit-car industry. Volkswagen made no secret of the older-style chassis construction, even showing a bodyless Beetle in one of its equally unique ads. (Volkswagen of America, Inc.)

The Beetle-based Cimbria SS stands 41 inches high, weighs 1,650 pounds total, and will move from 0 to 60 mph in 10 seconds, with a top speed of about 110 mph. (Amore Cars Ltd.)

certainly nothing to be ashamed of, and one popular Volkswagen ad of the 1960s even showed the chassis and seats without the Beetle body, over the headline, "Can you name this car?"

Obviously, what the Volkswagen works could bolt onto a chassis with eighteen bolts per side, someone else could unbolt and replace with another body of, shall we say, entirely different character. This was hardly a major discovery, but one of the first people to do anything about it was Bruce Meyers, the Californian (who else?) who started unbolting Beetles in the early 1960s, shortening the pan chassis a few inches, and bolting on peculiar little open, doorless bodies of fiberglass which came to be called "dune buggies." By the 1960s the Volkswagen was the only car left in the world to which something like this could be done with anything

even approaching simplicity. And people began to realize the partially obvious fact that, combined with emerging fiberglass technology, "What we have here, gentlemen, is no less than the second generation of custom coach building."

In essence, they were correct. The wheel had turned full circle and the car that personified uniformity now offered unlimited possibilities of originality and individualism. Unfortunately, the reincarnation of custom coach building *mit Beetles und "Fibreglas"* got off to a somewhat overenthusiastic and therefore bumpy start. The classic, basic dune buggy was a deceptively simple conversion. The body was doorless, topless, and completely comfortless—more of a bucket car than even the *Kübelwagen*. There really *was* little more than bolting a plastic fun body onto a Beetle chassis and

The Kelmark GT MK II is a convincing counterfeit of the Dino Ferrari, considered to be one of the most beautiful of contemporary sports cars. (Kelmark Engineering, Inc.)

Kelmark's GT is about as pure an example of the "unbolt the Bug; bolt on beauty" concept as you will find. The car can go from 0 to 60 mph in under nine seconds, and from crate to concrete in 30 hours. Motoring journalists regard it as a state-of-the-art kit car.

(Kelmark Engineering, Inc.)

Pre-assembled Fiberglass Body

Stock VW Gas Tank   Seating Capacity – 2 Persons

Hidden Spare Tire   Backbone Type Frame –
                                                          Integral Floor Pan

                                                    Trunk Capacity – 9.9 Cubic Feet

                                                          4-Speed
                                                          Transmission
Front Wheels –
14" x 7"

Tires – ER 60x14

Front Suspension –
Torsion Bar, Tube shocks,
Anti-roll Bar, Fully
Independent

                                                          German Air-cooled
Rear Wheels – 15"x 8½"   Engine

Tires – GR 50x15   Rear Engine / Rear Drive

Rear Suspension –
Torsion Bar, Tube Shocks,   Dual Brake System
Fully Independent

Blueprint for a three-way stretch between Italian spirit, German mechanics, and American ingenuity.
(Kelmark Engineering, Inc.)

KELMARK ENGINEERING	9-18-78
Kelmark GT – Specifications	41375

Weight – 1700 lbs.	Ground Clearance – 7"
Weight Distribution (F/R) – 40/60	Overhang (F/R) – 39"/38"
Wheel Base – 95"	Head Room – 37"
Track (F/R) – 58"/60"	Top Speed – 100+ MPH
Length – 174"	Mileage – 35+ MPG
Width – 73"	Handling – Superior due to low C.G., wide track,
Height – 45"	and ideal weight distribution

A near-perfect blend of hedonism and asceticism, the Kelmark conversion combines the glamour of a superstatus sports car with the practicality of a Volkswagen. As a bonus, the 450-pound, aerodynamically slippery body helps to account for 35 mpg and 100 mph.

(Kelmark Engineering, Inc.)

117

making some electrical connections, and every kid regardless of age coveted his very own dune buggy. For a while you could even order one from that ultimate arbiter of acceptability, the Sears, Roebuck catalog. But the possibilities were there for something much nicer than a bare bucket car. Those possibilities were for an exotic rear-engined super sports machine appearing to be just off the boat from an Italian *carrozzeria*, for a replica of a great classic of the twenties or thirties, and for dozens of specialties and oddities in between. Unfortunately, the problems and complexities lying between a Beetle owner and an exotic custom car increased in geometrical proportion to the attraction.

It all looked and sounded so deceptively simple; an old Beetle, a big crate dropped on the front lawn by motor freight, a few weekends in the garage, and—voilà—an ersatz SSK or a slightly phony Ferrari, After all, it's just a big brother to those little plastic model-car kits, isn't it? Well, a lot of people in the 1960s found out to their dismay that their backyard garages weren't custom coach builder's shops and they weren't the artisans and craftsmen of the golden age of the automobile. The result was that fiberglass kit cars got a bad name, largely because both maker and custom got a bit carried away.

Have things changed in the 1980s? The answer is yes, for several reasons. First, the industry has found its footing and is flourishing. Secondly, there have been some important advances in fiberglass technology and small-volume automobile construction. Thirdly, there is now a secondary or support industry of kit-car accessories from antique-style instrumentation to turbochargers which add substance, reality, and diversity. And, most important, people's conceptions of kit cars have become more realistic and sophisticated. Perhaps the atmosphere is best summed up by George Levin, the chief executive officer of Classic Motor Carriages, builders of Mercedes and Bugatti replicas and other vintage revivals, when he says, "We're not just selling cars, we're building an industry."

The heartbeat of that industry is variety. At this writing there are over one hundred kit cars available from American companies, and at least a quarter that many more from British makers. The vast variety of vehicles running with Beetle backbones is genuinely amazing. It would take a separate volume to catalog, describe, and illustrate them, but we can look at a few examples from the major categories of super sports cars, classic replicas, and specialties to see just how the lowly caterpillar—er, Beetle— metamorphoses into the beautiful butterfly.

Let's say your warm little nose is being deformed from pressing against the plate glass window of your friendly neighborhood Ferrari, Maserati, Lamborghini, Aston Martin, or

The Bradley GTElectric is a unique combination of a modernistic fiberglass sports car body mounted on a VW Beetle chassis. The Tracer I electric propulsion system is connected to the standard Beetle transmission. The GTElectric will reach 75 mph and has a range of 75 miles between charges. (Electric Vehicle Corporation, Palmer Lake Plaza, 6860 Shingle Creek Parkway, Minneapolis, Minnesota 55430)

Porsche-Audi dealer. Fifteen years ago it was a Raleigh racer in the window, but the price of thrills has gone up—way up—since then. Let's see, if you sell your Beetle, auction the house, mortgage the kids, and put your wife out on a shady street corner you might just make the down payment. But wait, that slick magazine ad says there's another way. You can keep your wife and kids and the house, if you'll settle for that Beetle hidden deep underneath the sexiest-looking body this side of the Folies Bergère. "Ah, come off it," you say, "that ain't no Beetle under there." You flip the page and there's a remarkably familiar looking guy in a garage remarkably like yours unbolting the body of a remarkably familiar insect-shaped car while a remarkably magnificent sports car body sits partially uncrated in the background. "Hey! I could . . ." And the salesman writes up another kit-car sale.

The car in the magazine ad might well have been a Cimbria SS, a super-exotic Italianate kit car from appropriately named Amore Cars, Ltd., guided by *il direttore* Joseph Palumbo. The Cimbria follows the pattern for the Beetle-based custom coachwork revival by laying a fiberglass body with a shape that would turn heads on the Via Veneto onto the VW pan chassis (although an alternate frame for V-6's and V-8's is available for true speed freaks). The Cimbria is the product of a small organization of dedicated craftsmen of the "quality versus quantity" school who are into their fourth-generation edition of the gull-winged traffic stopper, which is available as a basic kit at one of the most attractive base prices in the industry, in preassembled form, or as a complete car.

If you want to reincarnate your Beetle into a new and glamorous life but have some doubts about your own abilities to handle the nuts and bolts of the matter, or don't want to spend a year's worth of weekends working on it, the Kelmark GT MK II may be the answer. This car is a very convincing counterfeit of a Dino Ferrari (acknowledged

The Tiger roadster from Thoroughbred Cars of Redmond, Washington, is not a replica of any particular car but rather a composite of the styling of English sports cars of the 1930s. It is mechanically one of the most versatile replicars, using either VW or other components. Note the Beetle taillights faired into the 1930s-style fenders. (Thoroughbred Cars, Inc.)

as one of the prettiest contemporary sports cars) and it has earned a reputation as one of the best engineered and fastest kits from crate to concrete. One buyer made it to the road in thirteen hours, although the maker suggests thirty hours for street readiness and another seventy to ninety hours to complete the detail work. The Kelmark comes with conventional doors (which extend into the roof, Cadillac limousine style, for accessibility and increased rigidity) hung on stock Pinto hinges and complete with roll-up windows—thus avoiding one of the great bugaboos of do-it-yourself automobiles.

The car has been evolving for ten years, having started life as a V-8 special, and was reengineered as a Beetle-based car in 1974. It is about as pure an application of the "unbolt the Bug; bolt on beauty" concept as you will find. Nothing on the standard VW chassis has to be altered, and the 450-pound body even bolts into the original holes. Inside there's a handsome dash panel with VDO instruments

The Lindberg Line of replicars. R to L: Lindberg's A-36 Auburn supercharged speedster, Mercedes M-32 roadster of 1930s flavor, and a hot-rod version of the 1911 C-cab Ford truck. (Lindberg Engineering)

and a surprisingly spacious and luxurious interior that is anything *but* homemade (some big-timers should take note) and which even provides the smell of real leather, air conditioning, and other goodies if you get into optional extras. The Kelmark GT MK II is regarded in the industry as a state-of-the-art car. It is probably the closest thing to a factory car if you are adventuresome enough to consider a kit car for everyday use. It is, perhaps not coincidentally, built in Michigan, and despite its Italian spirit and German soul there is a definite American "can do" quality about it. Its makers mean business; they have their own nationwide delivery system and they'll talk directly to your banker about financing. (They even got their product into the NADA value manual.) And, they'll also sell you a showroom model if you're short on Saturday afternoons.

Bradley Automotive, Inc., is what managerial types like to call a well-diversified enterprise. It is one of the oldest

and largest kit-car companies, starting out with the Bradley GT in 1971, which was the first "live" kit car many people ever saw. If you saw one in the early seventies with its super-low forty-five-inch silhouette, scooped sides, and clear Plexiglas gull-wing doors, you weren't likely to overlook it. The fact that you saw it at all was likely due to Bradley's innovative sales technique of recruiting its satisfied customers into a nationwide network of salesmen. Since those pioneer days the company's founder, Gary Bradley, says, "We've built up the company to where we now have the financial strength and the quality product to be recognized as a car manufacturer and not just 'another one of those kit car outfits.'"

In keeping with the manufacturer image, Bradley now markets only through dealers, some of whom are becoming interested in the kit-car concept as a hedge against the dullness of ordinary cars from the major motorcar makers. Bradley says: "We get ten to twelve thousand letters a month

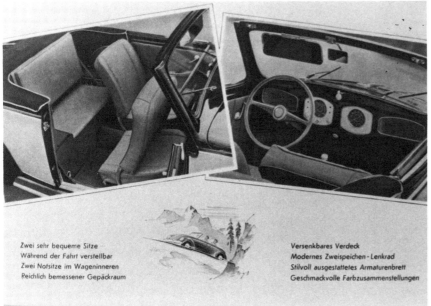

Zwei sehr bequeme Sitze —
Während der Fahrt verstellbar
Zwei Notsitze im Wageninneren
Reichlich bemessener Gepäckraum

Versenkbares Verdeck
Modernes Zweispeichen-Lenkrad
Stilvoll ausgestattetes Armaturenbrett
Geschmackvolle Farbzusammenstellungen

Ein Gedicht

Formschön
Elegant
Faszinierend
Temperament...

Mit Recht hat das *Cabriolet* viele Fre...

denn es bietet Ihnen zu jeder Zeit das Schönste:
Freude an Sonne und Bergen,
angenehme Geborgenheit bei Wind und Wetter.

Original sales brochure for the Hebmüller custom Beetle, circa 1949.
(Courtesy Elmer Kadar, Vintage Volkswagen Club of America)

The idea of making a Volkswagen into something a bit different from the run-of-the-factory Bug was not born with California kit cars. In 1949–50 the German coachwork company Hebmüller modified a Beetle into a sort of sporty cabriolet or everyman's gentleman's carriage. About seven hundred Hebmüller Beetles were built before the plant burned in 1950. The specials were sold through Volkswagen dealers, and today are Volkswagen collectors' dream cars.
(Volkswagen of America, Inc.)

from people." And, like his big brothers in the industry, Bradley believes that a wide range of models is essential to customer interest. So the original GT has been joined by the GT II, a more muscular-looking design which more than casually suggests the vaunted but never commercially produced Mercedes C-111 Wankel-engined prototype. Naturally, this end-of-the-millennium looking machine still sits on the old faithful Beetle chassis. Although there is now one shocking change—you can also have the Bradley GT II as an *electric* car called the GTElectric which will reach 75 mph and run for 75 miles between charges.

Bradley sees the 1980s as the decade in which the kit car will become a commonplace on the American automotive scene, and in preparing for that the company has answered one of the eventually asked questions about Beetle-based kit cars: "Since the Beetle is no longer marketed in the U.S., what happens when the supply of good or reconditioned Beetle chassis gives out?" The company has met

this problem by negotiating a contract with Volkswagen to import brand-new chassis from the Brazilian plant, where the Beetle is still big business, suggesting that the Beetle will have a lease on life for a long time to come. The company has also convinced major insurance companies that Bradleys are cars rather than contraptions, and are thereby entitled to competitive insurance rates.

If the rebodied-Beetle concept means anything, it means unlimited versatility and freedom of choice; for some people small, fast, ultramodern two-seaters are not their cup of tea. Instead, they long for what has been called the golden age of the automobile of the twenties and thirties: long flowing fenders, great Gothic grilles, and generous slices of Gatsby and Garbo. Freed of the need for huge stamping presses or expensive hand hammering of steel panels, fiberglass technology has been virtually a time machine to transport drivers back to the age of classic grace. Classic reproduction is one of the most attractive and appealing

The Bradley GT II Electric is a more muscular Beetle-based sports car resembling the Mercedes C-111. (Electric Vehicle Corporation)

Bradley GT Sport Electric was one of the first kit cars that many people saw "live." Its scooped sides, forty-five-inch-high silhouette and clear Plexiglas gull-wing doors created instant attention.
(Electric Vehicle Corporation)

parts of the reborn-Beetle phenomenon, and it is now possible to create whole traffic jams of "vintage" vehicles from World War I-era Model T trucks to Bugatti or Alfa Romeo racers of the twenties, to Mercedes-Benz 500 Ks of the thirties, and on to MG TCs and TDs of the fifties—even a replica of the 1957 Ford T-Bird if you're nostalgic for *American Graffiti.*

If you have yearnings for the cars of "the good ol' days" they will eventually lead you to Buffalo, New York, and the offices of Antique & Classic Automotive, Inc. If you've haunted the car shows like the great one at Hershey, Pennsylvania, there will be a definite sense of *déjà vu* about this place, a step into the great and glittering past of thoroughbred sports machines. Actually, the selection of replicas suggests a prewar British "motorcar purveyor,"

The Bradley Classic Marlene Electric is a Beetle-based replica of what may well be the most beautiful sports roadster of all time, the 1934 Mercedes-Benz 500 K. (Electric Vehicle Corporation)

Bradley's Baron is inspired by the 1929 SSK Mercedes-Benz, a popular subject for replicators since the late 1960s. (Electric Vehicle Corporation)

A favorite haunt revisited. In 1980 Bradley introduced a replica of the MG TD—Beetle-based, of course.
(Electric Vehicle Corporation)

James Bond's favorite 1930 "Blower Bentley" is replicated by Antique & Classic Automotive, Inc., of Buffalo, New York, for Beetle owners who want to relive the days of the legendary Bentley Boys. (Antique & Classic Automotive, Inc.)

Glimpses of a golden age of classic motor sport; (right) the much-loved 1927 Bugatti Type 37 B, and (left) the 1931 Alfa Romeo racer. (Antique & Classic Automotive, Inc.)

The idea of an affordable but good sports car was practically the invention of Sir William Lyons, and that idea produced the SS-100 replicated here by Antique & Classic Automotive, Inc. The idea was carried on to found the Jaguar family of cars.
(Antique & Classic Automotive, Inc.)

The Frazer Nash was a cult car for English sports car fanciers in the 1920s and 1930s. This 1934 Sports Tourer replicated by Antique & Classic Automotive, Inc., was originally a six-cylinder twin-cam car of 1600 cc displacement, and now lives again atop a Beetle chassis.
(Antique & Classic Automotive, Inc.)

BGW Ltd.'s Special Delivery utilizes Beetle doors and fenders and greatly simplifies conversion by leaving much of the original Beetle in place to save time and money. (BGW, Ltd.)

BGW Ltd.'s line now includes three Beetle conversions which—uniquely—do *not* require the Beetle body to be unbolted from the chassis. Right to Left: The VW Speedster (reminiscent of the legendary Porsche Speedster of the early fifties), the 1940 Willys Opera Coupe, and the Special Delivery mini panel truck.

BGW, Ltd.'s VW Speedster is a conversion that leaves the Beetle still attached to its chassis but modifies existing sheet metal with fiberglass replacements. (BGW, Ltd.)

perhaps like the firm of Charles Jarrot & Letts, Ltd., at 40–41 Conduit Street, London, where sports-minded drivers came to buy a Bugatti or to seek the advice of veteran race driver Charles Jarrot, who was racing automobiles when Victoria was still on the throne. Antique & Classic Automotive, Inc., offers the cream of British sports machines of the 1930s: a snarling cat in the person of the first Jaguar, the 1937 SS-100; the English gentleman's sporting carriage, the 1934 Frazer Nash; and James Bond's choice, the 1930 "Blower Bentley." And, if you want something still more sporting, with tiny fold-down Brooklands racing windscreens, how about a 1927 Type 35 B Bugatti or a 1931 Alfa Romeo racer? All legends in their own time, and revived in ours with the help of another kind of legend—the Beetle.

If shuffling off to Buffalo is too far, or too cold, you might try the little California town of Tollhouse at the foot of the Sierras. There a fiberglass artisan named Bob Lindberg offers the Lindberg Line, which includes an eye-filling replica of the 1936 Auburn supercharged roadster, a "drophead" roadster of early thirtyish flavor loosely patterned on a Mercedes but which from the rear is more suggestive of a Rolls 20/25. And, just for fun, there's a hot-rodded version of—of all things—a 1911 C-cab Ford truck!

If you're somewhere in between New York and California you could drop in on Bradley Automotive, Inc., in Plymouth, Minnesota (those guys who have a pipeline into the Brazilian Beetle connection, remember?). At one fell swoop in 1980 Bradley introduced four classic revivals: a 1929 Mercedes SSK roadster (a popular car with replicators since Brooks Stevens introduced the Corvette-based Excalibur SS in the late 1960s), a sleek and elegant 1934 Mercedes 500 K roadster, a 1952 MG TD, and a 1957 Ford T-Bird. (Yuk. Is 1957 "vintage" *already*?)

Is there *anything* that isn't replicated in fiberglass over a Beetle chassis? Well, so far nobody's had the audacity to replicate a 1959 Cadillac, but just about everything else

Not all custom-built Beetles come from a crate; there are still some *pure* do-it-yourselfers left. Frank Gregorius of Lake Cachuma, California, spent a year's worth of weekends and $350 to build *Genevieve* from a 1956 Beetle chassis, a 1963 Beetle engine, and other parts from such divergent sources as aluminum saucepans, brass doorknobs, and stray parts from a boat dock. *Genevieve* served as her creator's wedding limousine, and despite offers of orders for copies she will remain a Beetle original. (*Small World*)

is available. Omna-Auto, Inc., of Seattle, Washington, offers a cute-as-a-Bug Rumbleseat Roadster straight out of nineteen-aught-six with a pickup truck to match. The same company offers a half conversion which keeps the Beetle front, cuts off the rear half, and replaces it with a very neat and factorylike panel truck body called The Bugbox. Perhaps the wheel came full circle with a rather familiar-looking little utility vehicle from Hadley Engineering, Inc., of Costa Mesa, California. It bears, shall we say, a distinct resemblance to a certain general-purpose vehicle circa 1944 whose *GP* designation quickly corrupted to *Jeep*. In fact, the resemblance was so distinct that American Motors Corporation sued Hadley to keep them from using the entirely natural merger of *VW* and *Jeep* into *Veep*. So now, if you want one, it's a *Scamp*.

The Complete Guide to ...
VW BEETLE ENGINES, CHASSIS & SUSPENSIONS

©Auto Logic Publications, Inc., The Complete Guide to Kit Cars, P.O. Box 2073, Wilmington, DE 19899.

Year	Chassis #	Engine Series	Displacement	Horsepower	Voltage	Front Suspension	Rear Suspension	Special Features
1961-1965	3-192-507 to 6-502-399 and 115-000-001 to 115-979-200	Series D	1200cc	40	6 volt	Link and King pin	Swing Axle	All gears synchromeshed
1966	116-000-001 to 116-021-298	Series F	1300cc	50	6 volt	Ball Joint	Swing Axle	Dimmer switch mounted on steering column
1967	117-000-001 to 117-844-892	Series H	1500cc	53	12 volt	Ball Joint	Swing Axle	Dual brake system introduced with front and rear independent brakes. Two speed wiper system.
1968	118-000-000 to 118-1-016	Series H	1500cc	53	12 volt	Ball Joint	Swing Axle	Collapsible safety steering column-Automatic-Four lug wheels-3-point seat belt-Emission control.
1969	119-000-001 to 119-1-093-704	Series B	1500cc	57	12 volt	Ball Joint	IRS double jointed axle	Introduced combination steering wheel ignition lock
1970	110-2000-001 to 11-0-3096945	Series B	1500cc	57	12 volt	Ball Joint	IRS double jointed axle	
1971	111-2000-001 to 112-3200-000	Series AE	dual port 1600cc	63	12 volt	Ball Joint	IRS double jointed axle	Increased horsepower
1972	112-2000-001 to 112-3200-000	Series AH (Cal.) Series AE	dual port 1600cc	63	12 volt	Ball Joint	IRS double jointed axle	Wiper switch on steering column, modified choke, lower compression ratio. Pistons have recessed crowns. Modified muffler for faster preheating.
1973	113-2000-001 to 113-3200-000	Series AH (Cal.) Series AK	dual port 1600cc	63	12 volt	Ball Joint	IRS double jointed axle	Safety interlock seat belts. Modified exhaust gas recirculation. TDC sensor flywheel.
1974	114-2000-001 to 114-3200-000	Series AH (Cal.) Series AK	dual port 1600cc	63	12 volt	Ball Joint	IRS double jointed axle	Alternator replaces generator. Energy absorbing bumpers. Improved transmission mounts.
1975	1152-000-001 to 1352-000-001	Series AJ	dual port 1600cc	63	12 volt	Ball Joint	IRS double jointed axle	Electronic fuel injection-Alternator with integral regulator-New heat exchangers. Single tailpipe. Larger exhaust valve stems.
1976	1162-000-001 to 1362-000-001	Series AJ	dual port 1600cc	63	12 volt	Ball Joint	IRS double jointed axle	Automatic stickshift discontinued.
1977	1172-000-001	Series AJ	dual port 1600cc	63	12 volt	Ball Joint	IRS double jointed axle	

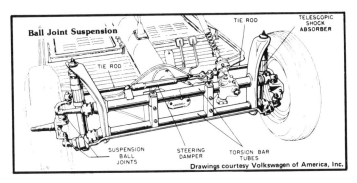

Ball Joint Suspension

TIE ROD — TELESCOPIC SHOCK ABSORBER

TIE ROD

SUSPENSION BALL JOINTS — STEERING DAMPER — TORSION BAR TUBES

Drawings courtesy Volkswagen of America, Inc.

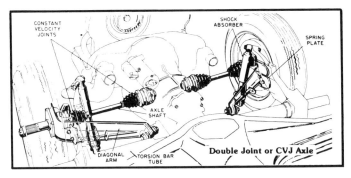

CONSTANT VELOCITY JOINTS — SHOCK ABSORBER — SPRING PLATE

AXLE SHAFT

DIAGONAL ARM — TORSION BAR TUBE

Double Joint or CVJ Axle

Front Suspension

King and Link Pin

In the king and link pin front suspension, the steering knuckles are fastened to the torsion bar trailing arms. Horizontal link pins locate the knuckle on the king pin. Though this system is durable, its roadholding ability leaves something to be desired, particularly in crosswinds.

Ball Joint Suspension

This arrangement uses horizontal torsion bars in two tubes to provide spring suspension. The steering knuckles are attached to the torsion arms by maintenance-free ball joints. These are pressed into the arms and have threaded pins which are secured to the knuckles by nuts. The upper ball joints fit in eccentric bushes with which the camber can be adjusted. The movement of the ball joint in the socket allows the wheel to more accurately follow the road surface.

Rear Suspension

Swing Axle

In a swing axle rear suspension, the rear wheels are sprung independently. Road shock is transmitted to the torsion bars by a trailing spring plate on either side of the rear axle. The drawback to this setup is that during hard cornering, the force against the outside wheel and the centrifugal force of the car causes the outside wheel to take on a great deal of positive camber. This force is relayed to the transmission where the axle pivots, causing the car to rise in the rear, resulting in oversteer and unstable handling. This flaw can be minimized by adding rear sway bars and diagonal trailing links (also called rear-axle locators).

Double Joint or CVJ Axle

In 1969 (1968 for automatics) VW sedans were first equipped with a double jointed rear axle. Both the drive shafts have two joints—one on the transmission case, one on the wheel. The rear wheels are mounted on trailing and diagonal links which attach to and pivot on the frame. The lateral forces which previously acted on the gearbox are now taken up by the diagonal links and transmitted to the frame, eliminating the center jacking that occurred with the swing axle. Roadhandling is improved because the outer joint maintains proper rear wheel camber, regardless of vehicle loading.

The VW Engines

Both the 36 and 40 hp engines are identical except for displacement and compression ratios. The 1500cc was the first Beetle engine with the 12 volt electrical system which allowed better lighting and more accessories. This engine can be mated to the 6 volt transmission by installing a 12 volt starter bushing in the transmission case and slightly enlarging the inside of the bell housing to accommodate the 12 volt flywheel. Dual port cylinder heads, which improve the intake flow, can be installed on any engine ('66 or later) by adding dual port intake manifolds.

Beetle specifications over the years are important when considering a new body on an old VW chassis.

(Auto Logic Publications, Inc.; *The Complete Guide to Kit Cars*, P.O. Box 273, Wilmington, Delaware 19899)

If you're a little shy about "taking it all off," you might consider the interesting reborn Beetles built by BGW, Ltd., of Milwaukee, Wisconsin, which let you take off just *some* of your Bug. BGW's Econo Rod concept is built around the idea that you don't have to take the Beetle off its pan to get an interesting custom Bug. For example, if you cut away the rear quarter panel of any Bug, including the Super Beetle, which is not often used in conversions, and epoxy on a fiberglass section supplied by BGW Ltd. (at a fraction of a whole car kit price) you get a neat little vintage panel truck which can be used straight or customized. A Forty Ford hood completes the retrogression. Or you can epoxy on a tiny dual rear window 1940 Willys "opera coupe" lid for a touch of *The Dead End Kids* or *The Bowery Boys.* Or, if you're not deep into Americana nostalgia and are more

the Continental type, there's a very mean looking Volkswagen Speedster, a creative blend of Bug and the 1955 Porsche low-slung Speedster. Aside from a unique flavor, the advantages of BGW, Ltd., conversions are that the design does not unbolt the Bug but preserves the original structural integrity and utilizes the original doors and fenders to substantially reduce conversion costs (and work), while giving a dramatically different perspective.

The list of Beetle-based replicas is virtually endless; to paraphrase Henry Ford, you can have most any car you want—provided it's a Beetle. You might say that the kit-car concept has succeeded in making a silk purse out of a sow's ear—or a Beetle's bottom—but then, as Beetle ads used to say, "Ugly is only skin deep," and in the end it's what's underneath that counts.

Besides serving as the chassis for all sorts of rebodying projects, the venerable and versatile Beetle chassis has long been the heart of a series of mini-Grand Prix cars which have competed all over the world in their own special Formula Vee (Volkswagen) class. Formula

Vee racing had served to bring fantastically expensive Grand Prix-style racing down to a Beetle-sized price, and has given many drivers a chance at the speedy single-seaters who would otherwise never have tasted even a chance at the checkered flag.

8/Götterdämmerung...Almost

Sic transit gloria mundi. The 1977 Beetle was the last of its kind to be sold in the U.S., and the effect on Americans was something like being told the truth about Santa Claus. But at least he went out in style—metallic paint, sports-type steering wheel, computerized fuel injection, heated rear window, four-wheel independent suspension, and a plug-in socket that could be connected to a computer for electronic service analysis.

The first rumblings came in the motoring press suspiciously close to the first fuel crisis. Editors began to wonder in print about a possible or even probable successor to the Beetle, which was a little like speculating on a successor to Sherlock Holmes, Mickey Mouse, or Santa Claus. It was kind of an unthinkable thought which, if forced, produced a "does not compute" response. The Beetle is the Beetle and that's that. But several kinds of realities were nibbling away at the legend.

By 1973 the Beetle was over thirty, supposedly cause for suspicion among a certain coterie of the little car's clients, and it was even more suspicious to automotive engineers, who still found it inconceivable that a pre-WW II anachronism could be successful in the space age despite Wolfsburg's unrelenting perfectionist pursuit of getting the bugs out of the Bug. There were, of course, *other* Volkswagens, including the 1500 knotchback in 1961 and the 1600 fastback in 1965, but they were still rear-engine air-cooled cars which showed their Beetle heritage clearly. Sooner or later a *new* Volkswagen had to be born, and some events far away from Wolfsburg were happening to induce labor pains.

The Beetle was a one-man car; it couldn't have been more so if the name "Ferdinand Porsche" had been stamped on every nut and bolt. Certainly Heinz Nordhoff deserves the credit for popularizing and perfecting the Beetle, but Porsche *invented* it—single-handedly. And in the early 1970s the time for one man's mark on an entire car was past. The age of individualist engineers like Ferdinand Porsche, Ettore Bugatti, Fred Duesenberg, W. O. Bentley, or Sir Henry Royce was gone. Of the great names only *Il commendatore*, Enzo Ferrari, could still sit behind the wheel of his "own" car. So there would be no new Beetle in the original sense; the Son of Beetle would be a computerized and calculated conglomerate of contemporary technology. Perhaps not as glamorous a way to create a car, but a more effective one. (*How* effective was something Japanese automakers were already beginning to demonstrate, to the consternation of Wolfsburg as well as to the more perceptive in Detroit.)

The suspicions and speculations of motor writers were fed and then confirmed by a peculiar-looking little car seen scudding around the Volkswagenwerk proving grounds at Ehra-Lessien and the back roads of Lower Saxony. It was coded as the EA 337, and some people called it the Blizzard (no puns about a snow job apparently intended). It was rigidly angular and, in some opinions, made the bulbous Bug look—oh, the irony of it!—*pretty.* The EA 337 was a synthesis of what European efficiency cars of the moment were about, and that meant front-engine, front-wheel-drive concepts as engineered by Fiat and Renault—the ecumenical influences of the Common Market and Pan Europa no doubt making it easier for German engineers to borrow from Latin technology. The speculators were finally vindicated when the fully developed EA 337 because the Golf* (following the Volkswagen tradition of naming new cars for the great winds of the world such as the Scirocco and Passat), and the

*German for gulf.

January 19, 1978, was the end of the endless lines of Beetles flowing from German factories. Production at Wolfsburg had ceased four years earlier (July 1, 1974), but continued at Emden and Hanover plants. After the last Beetle, Germans would ironically have to import from Brazil. (Volkswagen of America, Inc.)

car was marketed in the U.S. as the Rabbit. When the Golf/Rabbit was introduced in May 1974, the cover story was that it would be a companion to the Beetle, as other cars had before, and that while construction of the Beetle at Wolfsburg was yielding (without interruption) to the Golf, the old flagship would still be built at other Volkswagen plants in Emden and Hanover as well as several foreign plants. So on July 1, 1974, the last Wolfsburg Beetle—number 11,916,519—was built.

While this was a nostalgic and reflective moment for some, it was greeted with hope and anticipation by Volkswagenwerk executives who had watched Beetle sales slump in the European market and who worried that that eagle across the Atlantic who gobbled up a third of all their insect-shaped cars had lost his appetite for imported delicacies. The year 1974 was a landmark in another way; it marked Volkswagen's first loss, $200 million worth of unthinkable red ink. Whether it was the Beetle's fault or not, something had to be done.

There were, of course, other factors at work, more than merely the fact that the Beetle was "old-fashioned." The Beetle had started boring into the American market in 1949 at the now incredible-sounding price of $995, and pretty much held that line (allowing for then minimal inflation), rising only to $1,699 by its best sales year of 1968, when 423,000 emigrated to the U.S. It was genuine value for the dollar, all right, but after that the value of the dollar became progressively less genuine. Massive federal spending, the "Great Society," and LBJ's "splendid little war" in Vietnam had eroded the U.S. dollar, and when it was permitted to float in international exchange it proved to be waterlogged, particularly in comparison with the ebullient deutsche mark. Between 1968 and 1973 the once-almighty U.S. dollar lost 42 percent of its value against the deutsche mark, which automatically raised the price of German cars in America by nearly a half. The economy-king Bug was being undersold by domestic Pintos and Vegas, and like a storybook sea captain

Beetle sales in the U.S. were going down with the sinking American dollar. Beetle-style economy was becoming prohibitively expensive. And there were other problems. It became more and more difficult to accommodate emissions and safety standards of the 1970s to a car of the 1930s. Both the EPA and Ralph Nader saw the Bug as finally ripe for squashing.

In the U.S. that squashing of the Beetle in August 1977 was a little like the squashing of Jimmy Carter in November 1980; it was sort of expected, but the finality of it left a lot of people surprised. And, like that event of November 1980, it was cause in some quarters for lamentation and nostalgic yearning for a vanished past. *The New York Times* gave the Beetle an obituary fit for a minor head of state, praising his successful bucking of Detroit's system, his rise to become "one of the most familiar shapes on the planet," his amusing and memorable ads, his adoption as a symbol "for those who thumbed their noses at the establishment," and finally for his achievement of that rarity in motordom, becoming a legitimate piece of folklore, the like of which hadn't been seen since the Model A Ford and which may well never be seen again. The obit writer even remembered a few rusty VW jokes and then recalled, in perhaps the supreme simile, that "owning a VW was like being in love."

The *Times* piece set the tone for dozens of articles across the country in newspapers and magazines that usually left automobiles to the advertising department, with titles like "Requiem for a Lightweight" (*California*), "Beetle at the End of the Road" (*Daily Oklahoman*), "Fond Memories of Vlad the VW" (Fort Lauderdale *News & Sun Sentinel*), "Tears Are Falling for the Beetle's Demise" (Omaha *World Herald*), "Bug Bids Farewell to America" (*Temple Daily Telegraph*), "In Memory, Bug Will Live After Death" (*Daily Kansan*), and "Rest in Peace, Beetle" (*The New Republic*). An interesting percentage of the more "bereaved" articles originated in middle America, where the Beetle was originally rejected or at best tolerated as a suspicious foreigner. Later it became quite naturally adopted into the local fabric of the work ethic and respect for honest work, unpretentiousness, and enduring value, just as human foreign immigrants had earned acceptance a century earlier. Almost all of the articles and editorial comments reversed Marc Antony's eulogy speech for Caesar and seldom recalled things like the earlier Beetle's spartan heating system, its embarrassing windshield wipers, its placement of the fuel tank between the driver and harm's way, its leaflike behavior in crosswinds, the belated discovery that in high-speed collision its front seats needed reinforcement and the sad fact that in many cases the Beetle did not withstand traffic trauma very well. Instead, writers remembered Beetles through the golden haze of memory usually accorded graduation, a first kiss, the first semester at college, or a first apartment away from home—all painful but basically positive experiences which somehow become more so only with the passage of time.

History must record that the Beetle went out with more of a whimper than a wallop in its twenty-eighth year in the American market; only twenty-seven thousand were sold in 1977 as compared with nearly half a million only nine years before. When the last Beetles were off-loaded onto docks in Baltimore and Houston in the summer of seventy-seven an era ended, with only the Karmann Cabriolet convertible version being given a one-year reprieve (it took a while to coax a convertible Rabbit out of its hutch). The consolation for the bereaved was that three hundred thousand a year were still being cranked out in Latin and African countries, and even the Chinese are eyeing one of capitalism's most potent symbols for their own emerging motorization of the mainland. It has been said that production will continue as long as about five hundred people a day will buy Beetles around the world. Considering the ballooning population and the Bug's unique adaptability to the more inhospitable parts of this planet, that might mean forever.

Nor is the Beetle likely to evaporate from American shores like some windblown spring snowflake. Legends die hard, if at all. Human nature being what it is, as soon as the demise was announced people queued up to buy the last Beetles. An Oklahoma dealer reported that he could have sold his remaining cars at least four times over; a Detroit dealer couldn't get used to the idea that "there aren't going to be any more," and neither could his customers. Those who couldn't afford new ones at about four thousand dollars started fixing up their old ones, and in doing so started one more Beetle fad and created one more reverse status symbol—the restored Beetle.

A rare Hebmüller cabriolet in two-tone paint and a chuffle of "splits" at a Vintage Volkswagen Club of America meeting in California. (Bob Gilmore, VVWCA)

Less than three years after the official demise of the Beetle in the U.S., the phenomenon of resurrected Beetles was big enough business to attract the attention of *The Wall Street Journal.* The backyard economics of it all was sufficient to interest the Wall Streeter with a nose for preservation of capital and profit: a proven vehicle that could return a minimum of 25 mpg for an average investment of around $1,000, and not only with good resale value but even a likelihood of profit after use. In this economy that's enough to boost any family's personal Dow Jones. The fact is that recession, inflation, devalued dollars, and overvalued gasoline have reinfected growing numbers of people with old-style Beetlemania. Except this time they are haunting used car lots, classified ads, junkyards, and even dumps instead of showrooms to find not only restorable Beetles but recyclable Beetle parts—what in old-time mining parlance used to be called "reworking the tailings."

After you've found a beat-up Bug, what have you got and what can you expect to get? Well, if the engine is totally dead (usually unlikely) you could expect to pay around seven hundred dollars for a fully rebuilt one. An average amount of recycled parts and perhaps a paint job will put you in for over one thousand dollars, although do-it-yourselfers can cut the costs well below that. On the other side of the equation lies 25 mpg x 100,000 miles, the absence of car payments, and a sense of personal satisfaction at having beaten the system, something that has traditionally appealed to Volkswagen owners. To serve the homegrown Beetle builders a whole new industry has sprung up to supply the raw materials, both new and rebuilt. Perhaps the seriousness of the business is best measured by the latest "accessory" available from a California parts supplier—a complete new Beetle body fresh from a Mexican assembly line.

For a surprising number of people (dealers report that hardly anybody now trades in a Beetle on a Rabbit) all of this adds up as a viable answer to what are perceived

Among Volkswagen collectors the badge of honor is a split-window Beetle. Here, the president of the Eastern Region of the Vintage Volkswagen Club of America, Terry Shuler, poses proudly with his gleaming black lacquer 1949 split-window Beetle, number 1097328.
(Terry Shuler, VVWCA)

as unreasonable car and fuel prices of the 1980s. It is a new phenomenon for Americans traditionally accustomed to buying cars new and frequently, and one of concern to makers and dealers who realize that the smug owner of a restored Beetle (even if it is only a second or third car) is a customer out of the market for years. *The Wall Street Journal* quotes Terry Shuler, a Pennsylvania owner of several old Beetles, who concisely sums up the phenomenon: "You spend a few hundred dollars fixing up an old Volkswagen and you've got a car that will run forever. And you

The last American Beetle was the Karmann Cabriolet convertible,which continued through the 1978 model year, while Volkswagen tried to coax a convertible Rabbit out of the hutch. The open Bug with its rugged and luxuriously padded top in the vintage "grand style" was one of the best loved—and most prolific—convertibles ever built. The demise of the Beetle in the U.S. set off coast-to-coast lamentation and yearning for a simplistic and vanished past. *The New York Times* **ran an obituary fit for a minor head of state, and columnists across the country dredged up their personal nostalgia for their own beloved Bugs of days past. Even at its passing the Beetle could still conjure up its mystical, humanized attraction.**
(Volkswagen of America, Inc.)

get the same mileage as a new car without laying out $6,000 or $7,000."

Admittedly, Mr. Shuler has a small ax to grind. He is president of the Eastern Region of the Vintage Volkswagen Club of America, a group of devoted Beetlemaniacs who rebuild old Bugs both for everyday use and for the personal pleasure of preserving a piece of history—the same reason other people restore Chippendale desks, Kentucky long rifles, or Connecticut farmhouses.

So with some people driving restored Beetles because they are collectors, and others driving restored Beetles because they don't want to be collectors—of car-payment receipts—and others who are just letting their Beetles live out their natural longevity, and still others building and buying new Beetles by the hundreds of thousands each year in Mexico, Brazil, South Africa, and Nigeria, it is possible that the Beetle's demise, like Mark Twain's, has been a bit exaggerated. It may just be the longest *Götterdämmerung* on record, with the final glorious glimmer of sunset on permanent hold.

Index

(Volkswagen of America, Inc.)